The Hallé *1858-1983*

B

To my friends Arthur and Joyce Tennant

THE *Hallé*

1858-1983
A HISTORY OF THE ORCHESTRA

MICHAEL KENNEDY

 Manchester University Press

© MICHAEL KENNEDY 1982

All rights reserved

First published 1982
by Manchester University Press
Oxford Road, Manchester M13 9PL
and 51 Washington Street
Dover, New Hampshire 03820, USA

British Library cataloguing in publication data

Kennedy, Michael, *1926-*
  The Hallé 1858-1983.
  1. Hallé Orchestra—History
  I. Title
  785'.06'24733   ML1231

  ISBN 0-7190-0921-9
  ISBN 0-7190-0932-4 Pbk

Library of Congress Number 82 20830
Cataloging in Publication Data applied for

Photoset and printed in Great Britain by
Elliott Brothers & Yeoman Ltd., Speke, Liverpool

Contents

List of plates

*Photographs not otherwise credited are from
the archives of the Hallé Concerts Society*

Preface

In an ideal economic publishing world, it might have been possible to mark the Hallé Orchestra's 125th birthday as I should have wished – by an enlarged and revised re-printing of my *The Hallé Tradition* which Manchester University Press published in 1960. To do so, however, would have meant that the book would have been so highly priced as to defeat its object. Instead, therefore, I have written this new, shorter book which, although it covers the whole of the Hallé's existence, concentrates on the fifty years from 1933 to today. Those who would like more detail about Hallé's and Richter's eras are referred to *The Hallé Tradition*, which is still on the shelves of the public libraries. Even so, there are some new and corrected facts relating to those years in this new book. In addition I have also been conscious that perhaps I dealt less than generously last time with Harty's contribution and I have tried to rectify this. *The Hallé Tradition*, of course, ended with the centenary season of 1957-8. In this book, the whole of Sir John Barbirolli's era is included, and I have treated the programmes of his twenty-seven seasons in a detail comparable with that accorded to his predecessors in *The Hallé Tradition*. A fuller account of his life may be read in the two biographies published after his death.

This book, I must stress, is not a history of music in Manchester. That is an undertaking which must await a period of more leisure. So those who seek comprehensive references to the development of the teaching colleges, the spread of broadcasting and the history of chamber music and opera in the city will not find it here. Nor have I attempted to solve any kind of sociological equation between the rise and decline of Manchester and the fortunes of the Hallé. I do not think they are necessarily equated, anyway, but those who wish to study the relationship between the orchestra and the municipality will find it outlined here and may draw a moral. Nor do I forget that, these days, two-thirds of the Hallé's concerts are given outside Manchester. But the Manchester programmes are the basis of each season, and I hope that the citizens of Sheffield, Bradford and other stalwart Hallé supporters will acknowledge that there has to be a limit to the amount of detail. Giving brief surveys of each season is bound to be a subjective procedure. If I have concentrated on new or unfamiliar works, or certain memorable performances, that is because I believe and hope that approach will interest the majority of readers. It does not imply that I do not realise that the large number of performances of Beethoven, Mozart, Brahms, Schubert and Tchaikovsky is what draws most people to concerts.

Recently I read this in an article by an admired colleague: 'Orchestras do not have histories, for history implies continuity whereas the life of an orchestra is an erratic succession of glorious moments amid many others less memorable.' That could only have been written by a London critic. I do not believe that any writer in Liverpool, Birmingham or Glasgow would fail to discern continuity in their orchestras' history. Erratic the moments of glory may be, but they are none the less real and none the less formative of the tastes of successive generations. To write the history of an orchestra is inevitably to concentrate on conductors, virtuosos and administrators. I am aware, however, that the really important people are the players themselves, hard-working, loyal, often underpaid, always long-suffering and – much more often than is acknowledged – inspired. This book is my tribute to those hundreds of Hallé players who have given audiences throughout the world so much pleasure.

In *The Hallé Tradition* I gave a long list of individuals whose help and advice had been invaluable to me. Re-reading it, I am saddened to realise afresh how many of them are now dead. Without all they told me and without the documents they lent me then, this new book could not exist. Special acknowledgment is due also to Mr Clive Smart and Mr Stuart Robinson of the Hallé Concerts Society for constant help and encouragement, to Mrs Philip Godlee and Mrs J. H. Thom for the gift of their late husbands' Hallé papers, to the Editors of the *Guardian* and *Daily Telegraph* for permission to reprint extracts from their newspapers, to Dr Joyce Bourne for help in research, to Mrs A. Wragg for typing the manuscript, to the Librarian of the *Daily Telegraph*, Manchester, for much help, to Miss Audrey Napier Smith, and to Mr John Banks of Manchester University Press for much assistance.

We must now all look forward to the Hallé Orchestra's 150th anniversary in the 2007-8 season. To bring this book up to date for that milestone will be a very pleasant task for an octogenarian and I have every intention of undertaking it. The 200th birthday, though, will need another chronicler.

M.K.

1—*Mr Halle's Band*

Manchester's musical history began in 1422 when provision was made for 'singing men' at the Collegiate Church of that day. Successive royal charters renewed this provision; and still today, in the Cathedral, the choral element in the services is given high importance, and the organist arranges a series of excellent choral and orchestral concerts. But the dim origins of the Hallé Concerts lie in the subscription concerts devised in 1744 as a 'cover' for the activities of supporters of the Young Pretender (Bonnie Prince Charlie). These concerts survived his disastrous rebellion and were supported by the owners of Strangeways Hall and Heaton Park. From 1753 three concerts a week for two months in the year were given in the Marsden Street Theatre, the city's first permanent playhouse. Then, in Daye's Coffee House, off Market Street, a group of amateur flautists met once a fortnight. The flute was the fashionable instrument of the day. From these meetings developed the Gentlemen's Concerts. Their popularity merited the building of a concert hall, the first (so it is said) to have been built in the North specifically for concerts. It was opened in September 1777 with a three-day festival during which Handel's pastoral masque *Acis and Galatea* was performed. The hall, in Fountain Street, seated 1,200 and was lit by gas chandeliers. Soon works by Corelli, Handel, Mozart and Haydn were being performed at the Gentlemen's Concerts and a second festival followed in 1785.

Even before railways facilitated travel, Manchester was on the itinerary of many of the international musical celebrities who visited Britain. Among them were the soprano Angelica Catalani (1780-1849) and the violinist Paganini (1782-1840). In the spring of 1825 the prodigy pianist and composer Franz Liszt, then aged thirteen, played in Manchester; his 'New Grand Overture', the prelude to a one-act opera *Don Sanche*, was performed there on 16 June 1825. Ambitious festivals were held in 1828 and 1836. Between these events, in 1831, a new hall was built for the Gentlemen's Concerts on what is now the site of the Midland Hotel and where had been a cottage with a garden which included a windmill (hence Windmill Street at the rear of the Free Trade Hall). These concerts now had a list of six hundred subscribers, with two hundred waiting to join. The opening of the new hall impelled a writer in the London periodical *Harmonicon*, which existed from 1823 to 1833, to describe Mancunians as 'constantly in advance of all other parts of the kingdom in their musical taste and knowledge', an early example of the famous saying 'What Manchester thinks today, the rest of the country thinks tomorrow.' That it was not hyperbole then may be deduced from the 1836 festival, for which Maria Malibran, the mezzo-soprano, was engaged. Malibran, then twenty eight years old, enjoyed acclaim and reputation comparable with those of Maria Callas one hundred and twenty years later. She sang the Rossini rôles of Rosina, Desdemona and Cinderella with legendary brilliance. At the 1836 festival she sang in oratorio in the morning concerts in what is now the cathedral and in secular concerts in the evening in the Theatre Royal, Fountain Street. It was at one of the latter, on 14 September, that she collapsed after vying in virtuosity in operatic duets with Maria Caterina Caradori-Allan. She had had a riding accident some months earlier and had not been well. Nine days later she died in the Mosley Arms Hotel, Piccadilly.

When the 1777 festival was held, Manchester was an obscure country town. In 1836 it was the thriving, smoke-blackened commercial capital of the textile industry, centre of enormous wealth, with imposing buildings being erected on all sides but with the concomitant squalor of the housing conditions of the poor. It was a cosmopolitan town: many foreign businessmen had settled there, bringing their cultural interests with them. Among the settlers was Friedrich Engels, whose study of the working-class conditions was source-material for his friend Karl Marx. German names famous in the history of Manchester – Behrens and Simon, for examples – began to appear in the annals of its affairs. But when Mendelssohn conducted *Elijah* in the Gentlemen's Concert Hall on 20 April 1847, Manchester had not yet seen its most famous immigrant, the man whose name is synonymous with the city's music. It was not until 1848, the year of revolution in Europe, that the German pianist Carl Halle, who had been living in Paris since 1836, fled to London with his wife and children.

Hallé (as he later became known, adding the acute accent to his name to ensure that the English did not pronounce it as Hall) was born in Hagen, Westphalia, in 1819. He was a musical prodigy, greatly gifted as a pianist. At the age of seventeen he went to Paris, where he became a pupil of the Irish pianist and composer George Osborne. He founded a chamber-concerts series and was the first to play all Beethoven's piano sonatas in the French capital. He became the friend of Liszt, Chopin, Wagner, Mendelssohn, Paganini and, especially and significantly, Hector Berlioz. (His *Autobiography* contains illuminating descriptions of Chopin and Liszt.) Parisian artistic society at that time was of a stellar magnitude, and Hallé was a focal part of it for twelve years. His playing was heard by a Manchester calico printer Hermann Leo (who lived at 39 George Street) on a business visit to France; and when Leo, a director of the Gentlemen's Concerts, heard that Hallé was in England in 1848 he invited him to settle in Manchester to take its musical education 'in hand'.

A typical Gentlemen's Concert of that era comprised a Haydn symphony, arias and duets by Rossini, Bellini and Donizetti, an Auber overture, and other pieces. Oratorios and extracts from Handel's works were regularly performed. Beethoven's first two symphonies and the Fourth and Eighth had been played. Michael Costa and Sir George Smart were occasional guest conductors, otherwise the concerts were sometimes led from the first violin desk by the Manchester musician C. A. Seymour or conducted by J. Z. Herrmann. Hallé arrived in August 1848 and was disgusted by Manchester's lack of appreciation of Chopin's playing at his dying friend's recital on the 28th. He was horrified by the poor standard of the orchestra when he played Beethoven's 'Emperor' concerto on 13 September and contemplated leaving immediately, but suddenly realised he was 'supposed to change all this'. So he set about doing so. He started chamber concerts in the Royal Manchester Institution (now the City Art Gallery), being joined in trios by the Moravian violinist Heinrich Ernst (1814-65) and the Italian cellist Alfredo Piatti (1822-1901), early instances of the high standard of player Hallé was able, as a result of his Paris years, to inveigle to Manchester. He founded a choir and, in September 1849, was offered the conductorship of the Gentlemen's Concerts. He laid down stringent conditions, which were accepted, and made his first appearance as conductor on 20 February 1850, in a programme which included symphonies by Haydn (unspecified) and Mozart (No. 40) and the Kyrie and Benedictus from Mozart's Requiem. Within a short time he transformed the playing and the programmes – and hitherto, it must be remembered, he had conducted scarcely at all. But he had studied both Habaneck and Berlioz at their Paris rehearsals – and obviously he was a 'natural'.

Hallé's industry and application were phenomenal. He taught himself English, copying sentences from newspapers and books to aid his progress. Within four years he was able to write programme-notes for his chamber concerts. He listed the works of major composers performed in Manchester in the five years before his arrival and he gradually expanded the orchestra's repertory. Beethoven was his first objective. In 1850 he conducted the Fifth and 'Pastoral' Symphonies, in 1851 the 'Eroica', Fourth and Eighth. Otherwise the programmes remained miscellaneous in character. There were only forty players and the only Berlioz work he conducted in his first decade was *Harold in Italy* in 1855. He gave piano recitals in Manchester and London and in the winter of 1854-5 was involved with the composer Edward Loder (1813-65) in a plan to establish an opera company in Manchester at the new Theatre Royal in Peter Street of which Loder had been musical director since 1851. The scheme foundered in the economic situation created by the Crimean War.[1]

In 1855 also, as Hallé's diary tells us, he was on the point of resignation from the Gentlemen's Concerts because some of his conditions had not been fulfilled. With the rebuilding of the Free Trade Hall to Edward Walters's splendid design in 1856, the opportunity for a larger orchestra playing to larger audiences presented itself and Hallé was approached in December 1855 to launch some private venture there. But he remained loyal to the Gentlemen's Concerts. Then, in 1857, came the ambitious Art Treasures Exhibition, held for six months from May to October on a site near what is now Old Trafford cricket ground. A Crystal-Palace-like pavilion was erected to house the twelve thousand exhibits. Hallé was invited to expand the Gentlemen's Concerts Orchestra to give concerts on the exhibition site and in the Free Trade Hall – concerts were given every afternoon but he conducted only on Thursdays. He recruited the extra players from London, France, Belgium, Germany, Holland and Italy, 'not without trouble', as he said. A letter dated 1 May 1857 from Frederick Chappell on behalf of the colourful conductor and impresario Louis Jullien threatened Hallé with legal proceedings for endeavouring 'to persuade several of the members of his orchestra to break their written engagements with him and to enter into new contracts with yourself . . . As a foreigner you are probably not aware that it is a criminal offence against the Laws of England to entice Servants away from their employment . . .' With the enlarged orchestra of only fifty-two players, nevertheless Hallé was able on 8 September 1857 to give the first Manchester performance of Berlioz's overture *Carnaval Romain* and on 8 October the first Manchester performance of Beethoven's Choral Symphony. When the exhibition closed Hallé could not face a return to his own small orchestra; he wanted to keep the large orchestra and so he 'determined to give weekly concerts during the

[1]Hallé conducted Beethoven's *Fidelio*, Mozart's *Die Entführung aus dem Serail* and *Don Giovanni*, Weber's *Der Freischütz*, Donizetti's *Lucrezia Borgia* and *La Favorita*, Meyerbeer's *Les Huguenots* and *Robert le Diable*, and others. When the management refused the insistence by Don Giovanni (Carl Formes) on a bottle of real champagne in the last act, Hallé supplied it from his own purse.

autumn and winter season at my own risk and peril, and to engage the whole band'. It is to the credit of the Gentlemen's Concerts committee that they did not forbid their conductor to launch private, rival concerts using many of their players – no doubt they believed the venture could not succeed. With the backing of Forsyth Bros., Hallé's orchestra of fifty-eight players gave its first concert in the Free Trade Hall on Saturday 30 January 1858, the programme including Beethoven's First Symphony and Weber's Concertstück in F minor, op. 79, with Hallé as solo pianist. It was a rainy night and the hall was not full, but Hallé was undeterred: 'I felt the whole musical education of the public had to be undertaken . . . The "Gentlemen's Concerts" were an exclusive society; none but subscribers were admitted and no tickets sold. Before my advent they had never even published the programmes of their concerts, and the directors had only done so since 1850 at my earnest request, because I objected to conducting concerts of this clandestine sort. To the public at large symphonies and overtures were therefore *terra incognita*, and it was not to be expected that they would flock to them at once.'

The first season of sixteen concerts made a profit of half a crown. Within ten years Hallé's profits amounted to £2,000. For the next thirty-seven years he conducted every Manchester season of his concerts, established a series in Bradford and took the orchestra to Bristol, Edinburgh, London and many other towns. 'Mr Hallé's Band' became part of the scenery in the North. He never abandoned his policy of cheap seats, for he was one of the great progressive educators of the Victorian era. Until the formation of Henry Wood's Queen's Hall Orchestra in 1895, London orchestras in the nineteenth century were mainly *ad hoc* bodies, sharing many of the same players. In Manchester, after 1858, there was for the first time in British history a professional symphony orchestra with a personnel which remained relatively unchanged. Constant rehearsal ensured well-prepared performances. At almost every concert Hallé not only conducted but usually was soloist in a concerto or contributed piano solos. His taste was catholic, his enterprise unflinching. He gave complete concert performances of operas such as *Fidelio* and *Die Zauberflöte* and of Gluck's *Armide*, *Iphigenia in Tauris* and *Orfeo*. He introduced nearly all the important contemporary works to the city within a short time of their first performances elsewhere – the symphonies and concertos of Brahms, Dvořák and Saint-Saëns, for example. He conducted the first performance in England of a symphony by Tchaikovsky – No. 5 on 2 February 1893. Verdi's *Requiem* was played within two years of its first performance. Hallé himself was soloist in Brahms's B flat concerto in

1882 when he was sixty-three, only its second British performance. The symphonies of Haydn, Mozart, Schubert and Beethoven were standard fare (in the 1870-1 season, to mark the centenary of Beethoven's birth, Hallé conducted the nine symphonies in chronological order and the Mass in D); the great choral works of Haydn, Bach, Handel and Mendelssohn were often performed, starting the Hallé Choir's important contribution to the concerts. Long extracts from Wagner's operas were given, with the orchestra increased to over a hundred players. But perhaps Hallé was proudest of his service to his friend Berlioz. In Manchester he conducted the first performances in Britain of the *Symphonie Fantastique* (9 January 1879), *La Damnation de Faust* (5 February 1880) and *L'Enfance du Christ* (30 December 1880). *Roméo et Juliette* was given in full on 29 December 1881. The outstanding soloists of the day appeared at the concerts – the violinists Joachim, Sarasate and Neruda, the pianists Pachmann, Fanny Davies and Hans von Bülow (Hallé and Bülow gave the first English performance of the two-piano version of Brahms's *Variations on a Theme by Haydn* on 12 February 1874), the cellists Piatti and Hugo Becker, the singers Jenny Lind, Albani, Lilian Nordica, Clara Butt, Sims Reeves, Edward Lloyd, Henschel and Santley. At a performance of Grieg's Piano Concerto, Hallé was the soloist while the composer conducted. When Hallé took his orchestra to London in the 1890s, Bernard Shaw compared it favourably with the orchestra which played at Hans Richter's London concerts, writing of 'the rare combination of intimate knowledge of their repertoire with unimpaired freshness of interest in it'. Throughout all these years, too, Hallé continued to conduct the Gentlemen's Concerts, now diminished in importance, played regularly in chamber music and gave piano recitals.

In 1888 Hallé was knighted. After his seventieth birthday in 1889 he pushed forward plans for the erection of a new concert-hall in Manchester especially to house his concerts. If it were to be built, he said, he would hand over the concerts (which were his private property) to a society. Alas, this scheme, which would have eased so many financial problems to this day, was abandoned because 'trade was too bad' to allow of a public appeal. Instead efforts were concentrated on fulfilling another ambition he had cherished since 1854, the establishment of a college of music where local talent could be trained. Thus was born the Royal Manchester College of Music, which opened its doors in October 1893 with Hallé as Principal and professor of pianoforte. He seemed ageless, indestructible. In 1888 he had married as his second wife the violinist Wilma Norman-Neruda.

Together they toured Australia twice and South Africa. On 25 October 1895, a few weeks after returning from South Africa and the day after he had rehearsed for the first concert of the 1895-6 Manchester season, he died suddenly. Thousands lined the streets for his funeral: nothing like it had been seen in Manchester since the death of John Dalton. By his own reckoning, in his thirty-seven years (which excludes eight at the Gentlemen's Concerts) Hallé had performed at his concerts 32 oratorios, 71 other choral works, 110 symphonies, 214 overtures, 205 miscellaneous orchestral pieces, 183 concertos and 'minor pieces without number'. Most important of all, he had transformed public taste. His early concerts were miscellanies, including ophicleide solos, operatic *pot-pourris* and popular ballads. After a few years, the programmes, though still alarmingly long, more closely resembled what is understood by the term 'symphony concerts'.

II—*Richter's era*

The continuation of Hallé's concerts was ensured by three Manchester businessmen, friends and associates of Hallé – Gustav Behrens, Henry Simon and James Forsyth – who guaranteed them for four seasons. Behrens determined that only the best was good enough for Manchester and immediately offered the post of conductor to the Austro-Hungarian Hans Richter, who at the time of Hallé's death was fifty-two and had been conductor of both the Vienna Court Opera and the Vienna Philharmonic Orchestra since 1875. At the age of twenty-three Richter had assisted Wagner in preparation of a fair copy of the score of *Die Meistersinger von Nürnberg*, had then conducted opera in Munich and Pest, and had conducted the first performance of Wagner's *Ring* cycle at the first Bayreuth Festival in 1876. In Vienna, he conducted the first performances of three of Bruckner's symphonies, of Brahms's Second and Third Symphonies, and of Tchaikovsky's Violin Concerto with Adolph Brodsky as soloist. Since his first visit in 1877 he had been an annual visitor to London, establishing his own series of concerts. In addition he had been conductor of the Birmingham triennial festival since 1885 and had conducted the first London performances at Covent Garden of both *Die Meistersinger* and *Tristan und Isolde*. He indicated his willingness to go to Manchester but was understandably anxious about securing his pension from the Court Opera post. It was four years before the Behrens–Richter negotiations were concluded, matters being complicated by the supplanting of Richter in Vienna in 1897 by Gustav Mahler. Anxious not to be accused of 'pushing out' so long-established a figure, Mahler doubled Richter's salary when a new five-year contract was offered and accepted in 1899; but Richter soon asked for it to be annulled because 'I no longer take any pleasure in the theatre'. Mahler later discovered that Manchester had offered Richter five times as much!

In the interregnum at the Hallé, Behrens engaged a series of guest conductors for the 1895-6 season, including Brodsky, who had been brought to Manchester in 1895 by Hallé to lead the orchestra and to be violin professor at the Royal Manchester College of Music. When Hallé died, Brodsky became Principal of the college and resigned the leadership post. For 1896-7 the bulk of the Hallé conducting was given to Frederic Cowen. In those days Hallé players also provided the majority of the personnel for the Liverpool Philharmonic Society's orchestra and Cowen was appointed conductor there and in Bradford. The Liverpool committee lost patience with Richter and were content to retain Cowen, but Manchester always made it clear that Cowen was a stopgap and dismissed him after the 1898-9 season. This led to considerable controversy and ill-feeling; the Cowen–Richter issue was the first crisis to be encountered by the Hallé Concerts Society, which was incorporated in June 1899. Cowen was, in fact, a good conductor (and a prolific composer). In his three Hallé seasons he conducted the first Manchester performances of Dvořák's Cello Concerto, Brahms's First Piano Concerto and Tchaikovsky's *Theme and Variations* and Violin Concerto (with Brodsky as soloist). In December 1897 he conducted a concert performance of Berlioz's *Les Troyens à Carthage*, comprising Acts 3, 4 and 5 of the opera *Les Troyens (The Trojans)*, and exactly a year later he conducted the first Elgar performance at the Hallé Concerts, the cantata *King Olaf* which Arthur Johnstone, the critic of the *Manchester Guardian*, said 'did not seem to make any great impression on the audience'.

Johnstone, a great critic who was to die in 1904 at the age of forty-three, was a firm supporter of the idea of bringing Richter to Manchester. 'To Richter's influence and example', he told his readers, 'far more than to anything else that could be named, is due that prodigious improvement in the standard of orchestral performance all over the world which is the most notable feature in the history of music during the past thirty years.' Richter conducted his first Hallé concert, beginning with the *Meistersinger* overture, on 19 October 1899, in the midst of the Boer War. Thus was inaugurated a decade in Mancunian cultural history which seems in retrospect like a golden age: Richter at the Hallé, Brodsky and the Brodsky Quartet at the college; Scott

Sir Charles Hallé: (*above*) in 1850; (*below*) conducting the orchestra in 1895, with Lady Hallé (solo violinist)

Two historic occasions: (*above*) Sir Charles Hallé (on rostrum, holding baton in both hands) watches the Prince and Princess of Wales (just below) opening the Royal Jubilee Exhibition in Manchester on 3 May 1887 at the old Free Trade Hall, before a performance of Mendelssohn's *Hymn of Praise*; (*below*) John Barbirolli's first Manchester concert at Belle Vue in August 1943 (both *News Chronicle/Daily Mail*)

editing the *Guardian*, with writers like Johnstone, Ernest Newman, Samuel Langford, C. E. Montague, Allan Monkhouse and James Agate; Miss Horniman's repertory company at the Gaiety; Backhaus, Max Mayer, Egon Petri, Marie Brema and Carl Fuchs among the teachers at the college; Lancashire's batting at Old Trafford opened by MacLaren and Spooner, with J. T. Tyldesley to follow, and Dean and Huddleston to open the bowling. Yet Richter's conductorship was marked and marred by controversy. There was a growing 'anti-foreigner' element, for one thing. And the Hallé committee were gradually made aware that they could not expect their conductor to conduct every concert everywhere, as Hallé virtually had done. The orchestra scattered to the seaside piers in the summer and if its conductor then went to Covent Garden, that was accepted. But when a group of London players broke away from Henry Wood in 1904, formed the London Symphony Orchestra and invited Richter to be its conductor, that was a straw in the wind. Soon, too, the critics, in the newspapers and among the guarantors, began to grumble about the conservatism of Richter's programmes. The names of Debussy, Ravel, Stravinsky and Delius were advanced and found no sympathetic echo with Richter. 'Too much chorus, too much ugly music, not enough good singers, apparently the programmes have been thrown together with a pitchfork': that was the burden of one complaint to the Hallé chairman in 1906. Newman, when he became *Guardian* critic, savagely attacked Richter performances; and Richter himself blundered in preferring to conduct at Covent Garden on the night of the Hallé's fiftieth anniversary concert in 1908. In January 1911 there was an organised demonstration against Richter in the Free Trade Hall when the solo violinist was applauded at excessive and embarrassing length. A month later Richter announced that he was to retire because of failing eyesight. This was true, but there is no doubt that his decision was precipitated by his critics. Of his twelve seasons, only four resulted in a monetary profit for the society.

Yet what would we not give to have heard Richter conduct Beethoven, Brahms, Dvořák and Wagner? Langford wrote of him 'Where music speaks the deepest truths it will remind us most inevitably of him'. Richter is forever associated with the music of Elgar, which he championed enthusiastically. Having conducted the first performance of the *Enigma Variations* in London in June 1899, he introduced them to Manchester, Liverpool, Bradford and elsewhere in February 1900. Thereafter Elgar's major orchestral and choral works were given regularly in Manchester under Richter's baton. Hallé players were in Richter's orchestra for the first performances of *The*

9

Dream of Gerontius, The Apostles and *The Kingdom* at the Birmingham Festivals of 1900, 1903 and 1906; the Hallé gave the first performance of *In the South* in London in 1904 and of the First Symphony in Manchester on 3 December 1908. The symphony was dedicated to Richter as 'true artist and true friend', and the occasion was a triumph for the work, the composer and the conductor.[1] Richter also included works by other British composers – Parry, Stanford, Cowen, Mackenzie, York Bowen and Cyril Scott – and he introduced one by one the great symphonic poems of Richard Strauss. He conducted the first English performance of a Sibelius symphony (No. 2 on 2 March 1905); he conducted the twenty-two-year-old Bartok's symphonic poem *Kossuth*; he introduced Bruckner's Third and Seventh Symphonies to Manchester, but nobody liked them; he conducted Liszt's *Faust Symphony* and *St Elizabeth*, Bach's *St Matthew* and *St John Passions*, Handel's *Messiah*. He brought superb soloists to the concerts – Casals, Ysaÿe, Ziloty, Lady Hallé, Agnes Nicholls, Petri, Busoni, Kreisler, Godowsky, Bartók and Dohnányi. He encouraged the composing aspirations of one of his cellists, J. H. Foulds, who went on to become an English Charles Ives. He conducted the orchestra's first pension fund concert. He lived in 'The Firs' in Bowdon and at Christmas would invite the players, in groups, to a meal there. He could out-eat any of them. Before a concert, he used to tell friends he was 'too excite' to eat. They would then watch him go through the menu, drinking a large bottle of burgundy with it! He was the stuff of which legends are made. He worshipped the three Bs (Bach, Beethoven and Brahms) and he himself was bearded, bulky and benevolent, albeit on the rostrum a martinet with a keen memory for players' previous errors!

---

[1] It is illuminating to record what the Manchester public was offered during this particular week: the Elgar symphony at the Hallé; on the next night Beecham conducting Delius's *Sea-Drift* and other contemporary works; French music at the Gentlemen's Concerts with Fauré playing in one of his piano quartets; the Carl Rosa Opera at the Theatre Royal, Edward Terry at the Prince's Theatre, a play by Charles McEvoy at the Gaiety, Vesta Tilley at the Palace, Kitty Loftus at the Tivoli. In the following week, 6-13 December, Busoni was at the Gentlemen's Concerts, Egon Petri at the Hallé, the Carl Rosa performed *Lohengrin* and *Don Giovanni* and the Vedrenne-Barker company gave Shaw's *Man and Superman* and *Arms and the Man* at the Prince's.

III—Balling and Beecham

If it was difficult to decide who should follow Hallé, it was no easier to find a successor to Richter. It is doubtful if the leading British contender, Henry Wood, was considered. Instead, members of the Hallé Committee set off for Garmisch to try to persuade Richard Strauss, but in vain. The 1911-12 season was conducted by a miscellany of guests, Wood, Elgar, Michael Balling, Oskar Fried, Franz Schalk, Sir Frederick Bridge, Landon Ronald, Ossip Gabrilowitsch, Percy Pitt and, on 7 March 1912, Thomas Beecham, whose programme included Grétry, Delius, Strauss and Mozart. But this was not Beecham's first Hallé concert.[1] That had been on 6 December 1899 at St Helens. His father, Sir Joseph Beecham, decided to mark the year of his mayoralty of the town by promoting a Hallé concert. Richter had to withdraw because he returned to Vienna to wind up some business there. Thomas, then twenty, proposed himself as substitute and, after initial misgiving, Sir Joseph supported him. The Hallé's leader, Risegari, refused to play under a novice, but Sir Joseph told the Hallé committee 'Thomas conducts or I engage a London orchestra'. Thomas conducted – successfully – the *Meistersinger* overture, Beethoven's Fifth Symphony, and extracts from *Lohengrin* and Berlioz's *La Damnation de Faust*. Beecham's Manchester début with the Hallé in 1912 was also not without controversy: the Dean, who was a member of the Hallé Society, 'feared for the moral tone of Manchester' because Beecham had recently been cited as co-respondent in a divorce case. He was concerned about the effect of 'this man of unclean life' on the ladies of the choir, but they appear to have been unscathed! (Beecham's first Manchester appearance as a conductor had been on 4 December 1908, the night after the first performance of Elgar's symphony, when he brought his New Symphony Orchestra and the North Staffordshire Choral Society to perform Delius's *Sea-Drift* and works by D'Indy, Reger, Holbrooke and Strauss. The audience was 'miserably small'.)

Before the end of the 1911-12 season the new Hallé conductor was announced. He was the German Michael Balling who at the age of forty-five had already had an eventful career, first as a violist, then

---

[1] In 1894, as a schoolboy at Rossall, he joined the percussion section when the Hallé took part in the school's jubilee concert.

founding a music school in New Zealand and conducting incidental music at Stratford-upon-Avon. He had conducted opera in Hamburg, Breslau and Karlsruhe – and at Bayreuth. In 1911 he conducted performances of *The Ring* in English in Edinburgh, Manchester and other cities. Balling is the 'forgotten man' of Hallé history but he should not be. He was the first Hallé conductor publicly (on 29 November 1912) to call for municipal aid to the concerts; he ensured that the orchestra was paid a six-month salary instead of a fee per concert; and he advocated the building of an opera house in Manchester, with a resident company to serve Liverpool, Leeds, Bradford and other centres. When war was declared in 1914, Balling was in Bayreuth and remained in Germany although he kept in friendly touch with Gustav Behrens. If he had been able to stay in Manchester, he might well have achieved his ambitions for the Hallé, which played well for him, from all accounts. His programmes in his two seasons were, like Richter's, German-oriented, but he was enterprising. He conducted Bruckner's Ninth Symphony and *Te Deum*, Mahler's First Symphony, Elgar's *Falstaff*, Ravel's *Mother Goose*, Holst's *Beni Mora*, and he brought back Verdi's *Requiem* which had not been performed in Manchester since 1889.

Behrens determined that the concerts should continue during the war. Elgar conducted the first programme of the 1914-15 season, Beecham the second and Ronald the third. Other conductors were Safonoff, the Hallé choirmaster R. H. Wilson, Cowen (now Sir Frederic) and Hamilton Harty. A breath of fresh air came with Beecham, a Mediterraneanisation of the programmes: Debussy's *Printemps* and *Nocturnes*, Delius's *Paris* and *Sea-Drift*, Berlioz's *Te Deum*, Stravinsky's *Firebird*. He intensified the de-Teutonisation process in subsequent seasons. Along came Ravel's *Daphnis and Chloë*, works by D'Indy, Borodin and Berlioz, and a concert performance of Glinka's *A Life for the Tsar*. Beecham's interest in the Hallé was principally as an adjunct to his operatic schemes. In 1916 and 1917 he conducted memorable opera seasons in Manchester, with the Hallé in the pit. He took up Balling's idea and offered, on certain conditions, to build an opera house for the city. A sub-committee was formed (of course), but before any decision was taken Beecham went bankrupt and withdrew from the musical scene. He had, incidentally, taken no fee from the Hallé throughout the war. Once again, as it faced the difficult post-war period with an orchestra dissatisfied with its salary system and at one point almost reduced to two contracted players, the Hallé committee had to find a new conductor. In the last wartime seasons, guest conductors had included Eugene Goossens, Albert Coates, and Harty.

Beecham and Coates were committed elsewhere and urged the appointment of Harty. Accordingly this forty-year-old Ulsterman took over the Free Trade Hall rostrum in October 1920.

This is the point at which one should record the demise of the Gentlemen's Concerts. They had continued under Hallé's guidance but they no longer had the importance of their early years. Richter conducted them for a time but eventually asked the directors to relieve him of this extra duty and Henry Wood took them over. When the Midland Hotel was built in 1902 the Concert Hall was demolished but a hall was provided in the hotel. In 1920, after a history of 150 years, they were discontinued.

IV—*Harty*

Under Harty the Hallé Orchestra gave about sixty concerts a year, twenty-two of them in Manchester. The link with the opera season was severed. Harty (who had first conducted the Hallé on 6 March 1913) made his name as a brilliant piano accompanist to singers, who included his wife, the soprano Agnes Nicholls. He was also established as a composer and his aptitude for conducting was noticed when he directed performances of his own works. His first task in Manchester was to raise the morale of the orchestra and to lift the standard of playing back to its pre-war consistency. Within three months of Harty's appointment, Langford wrote in the *Guardian* that 'we may feel once more that there is no place in the orchestra for any but an ambitious player'. For some years the Hallé had had rivalry in Manchester from the more popular concerts run by the impresario Brand Lane. After 1920 Lane frequently engaged the Hallé for these concerts and it is a tribute to Harty that in January 1921 Richard Strauss had very few criticisms to make of its playing of his music when he conducted the orchestra at a Brand Lane concert. (When Harty conducted *Don Juan*, his beat at the difficult start was so exact that 'the cascade of seven semiquavers that follow the downbeat sounded like a tornado'.)[1] Subsequently Sibelius, Bruno Walter and Koussevitzky conducted the Hallé at Brand Lane concerts in the Harty era, and in 1935 Furtwängler and the Berlin Philharmonic appeared in the series.

Under Harty, who was knighted in 1925, the Hallé gave its first

[1]Leonard Hirsch: 'Memories of Sir Hamilton' in *Hamilton Harty, His Life and Music*, ed. David Greer (Belfast, 1979).

13

civic-aided concerts (with five hundred seats for schoolchildren) in 1924, made its first recording for the gramophone, and made its first broadcast. Harty was opposed to the broadcasting of concerts, for he feared they would affect concert-hall audiences – he called the B.B.C. 'the amiable bandits of Savoy Hill' and something stronger when they enticed away some of his best players to the newly formed B.B.C. Symphony Orchestra in 1930. There is no question – and the re-issue of some of his recordings proves it – that he made the Hallé into the best orchestra in the kingdom and that the formation of the B.B.C. orchestra and of the London Philharmonic by Beecham in 1932 were London's reply to this northern supremacy. He was a splendidly controversial and witty figure. Women were now joining other symphony orchestras, but Harty would not have them in the Hallé – even the harpist was male, the great Charles Collier – and, using his privilege as a composer, he had outspoken views on certain composers and works. For example, he deleted Strauss's *Symphonia Domestica* from one season because he believed that 'respect for the genius of the composer' would not be increased by its performance. He ranked Berlioz above Wagner and supported his conviction by giving superb Berlioz performances, including revivals of *La Damnation de Faust, Les Troyens à Carthage* and *Roméo et Juliette*. He conducted the first performance in Manchester of the *Grande Messe des Morts* and the critics came from Paris to hear it.

He was criticised, as Richter had been, for unenterprising programmes,[1] but to contemporary eyes they look enticing enough. He championed the music of Bax, Moeran and Ireland and he conducted the first performance in England of Strauss's *Le Bourgeois Gentilhomme* suite. Vaughan Williams's *A Sea Symphony* and *A Pastoral Symphony* were introduced to Manchester by Harty, also Strauss's *Alpine Symphony* and several of the works of Sibelius. In November 1927 he conducted the first Manchester performance of Mahler's Fourth Symphony, following it on 27 February 1930 with the first performance in Britain of his Ninth Symphony and with *Das Lied von der Erde* on 11 December 1930. He quickly brought into the Hallé programmes Walton's *Façade* Suite No. 1, his Viola Concerto (with Lionel Tertis as soloist) and *Belshazzar's Feast*. Shostakovich's First Symphony had its first English performance under Harty in Manchester on 21 January 1932. Among choral works he conducted were Kodály's *Psalmus Hungaricus*, Rachmaninov's *The Bells*,

---

[1] I received a letter some years ago from a man who had been severely critical of Harty's programmes. He had then gone to work in Berlin in about 1930 and wrote to Harty to apologise, saying that, compared with Furtwängler's, his programmes were daring!

Glazunov's *The Kremlin*, Bantock's *Song of Songs* and Delius's *A Mass of Life* (a performance which the composer told Neville Cardus was the best he had heard 'but don't let Beecham know'). On 12 December 1929 Harty was the solo pianist while the composer, Constant Lambert, conducted the first public performance of *Rio Grande*. Harty had also been soloist, with Beecham conducting, in the first performance of his own Piano Concerto. The revised version of his *Irish Symphony* was introduced at a Hallé concert, and the Hallé gave the first performances of his famous Handel transcriptions, the *Water Music* on 18 November 1920 and the *Fireworks Music* on 25 October 1923.

It is sometimes forgotten that Harty was one of the great Elgar conductors. After the Hallé had played the Second Symphony in London on 24 January 1930, Bernard Shaw described it to the composer as 'a stupendous performance . . . H. H. was a dripping rag at the end; but he had mastered and was feeling every phrase . . . As to that fortissimo in the rondo, which is like nothing else on earth (Beethoven nowhere!) you should have heard it. *I* never heard it before[1].' Harty's insight into Elgar is apparent from his 1932 recording of the *Enigma Variations* and even more from his 1930 recording of the Cello Concerto where his rapport with the soloist, his close friend W. H. Squire, makes for an especially sympathetic interpretation. When he first took over the Hallé, Harty had hoped for a new Elgar work for Manchester but had received a typically sour piece of Elgarian disillusion in reply to his request: 'I should think the good people there would be more surprised than pleased if you produced a new work of mine.' Harty conducted *The Dream of Gerontius*, *The Apostles* and *The Music Makers* in Manchester and was, of course, responsible for inviting Elgar, in the year of his seventieth birthday (1927) to conduct a programme of his own works including the Violin Concerto in which Brodsky, at the age of seventy-five, was soloist, emerging from retirement for the occasion. Elgar came once again, on 26 January 1933, to conduct *Gerontius*. Already a sick man, he sat in a chair to conduct a performance that is still recalled, after fifty years, by those who were privileged to be there.

While Harty was with the Hallé, the high standard of soloists was maintained. Among the violinists were Heifetz, Huberman, Szigeti, d'Arányi, Thibaud, Elman and Ysaÿe. Casals, Cassado and Suggia were solo cellists. The pianists included Schnabel, Cortot, Backhaus, Busoni, Gieseking, Haskil, Myra Hess, Josef Hofmann, Horowitz,

[1]Quoted in Percy Young: *Elgar OM* (London, 1957) pp. 377-8.

Rachmaninov, Rubinstein, Ziloty, Solomon and Rosenthal. It is said that Backhaus's 'greatest wish' was that he could afford to engage Harty and the Hallé to accompany him at all his concerts. Schnabel's performance of Brahms's B flat concerto was the occasion for one of the best Harty anecdotes. Schnabel missed out two bars in the finale and Harty quickly covered the memory lapse, so swift was his collaboration with the orchestra. Afterwards, Schnabel told Harty he thought the Hallé was almost as good as the Berlin Philharmonic. 'They're better', replied Harty, 'they play two more bars of the concerto!' All the leading singers of the day sang at the Hallé concerts, but one especially was associated with Harty. On 17 November 1921 the soprano soloist in Casella's *Venetian Convent* was Bella Baillie, as she was then known. Thus began the great career of Dame Isobel Baillie. It was to her, at an early rehearsal of *Messiah*, that he said: 'Go away. Read the words. Read them over and over until you mean every syllable of them. Then you will be able to sing.' She never forgot the lesson. Until the early 1960s her singing in *Messiah* at Belle Vue was a highlight of the Hallé season.

Most of the players in Harty's orchestra adored him. They felt that, at rehearsal, he was watching each one of them all the time. He never raised his voice, but explained exactly what he wanted and then gave an unequivocal beat so that his wishes were carried out – only thus could he have obtained such results on one rehearsal. He never sang or hummed, but whistled with perfect intonation and pitch. Some of the most illustrious names in Hallé history played in the orchestra during his régime: his leaders were Arthur Catterall, John Bridge and Alfred Barker, and among other violinists were Thomas Matthews, Laurance Turner, Philip Hecht, Clifford Knowles, Reginald Stead and Leonard Hirsch; Frank Park was his principal viola and the cellos were led by Clyde Twelvetrees and later by Stuart Knussen. At various times the woodwind included Archie Camden (bassoon), Harry Mortimer (clarinet), Alec Whittaker (oboe), Joe Lingard (flute) and the trombone section of Holt, Old and Hoyland has probably not been surpassed. Until his death in 1929 Willem Gezink was the timpanist. Well as Harty conducted a wide range of composers, it was in Berlioz, and especially in the *Symphonie Fantastique*, that he seems to have made his most powerful impression. Leonard Hirsch, a former Hallé violinist, in a memoir already quoted, has written that 'at the very opening of the work members of the orchestra had a very strange, inner feeling that, somewhere around them, was the presence of the great composer himself . . . Harty had such an incredible insight into the composer's mind that he seemed to be re-creating the very spirit of Berlioz before us'. He was also an exceptional interpreter of Brahms – both Langford and Cardus thought him unsurpassed in this composer's music. Where Brahms had previously often been played in a heavy, sluggish, academic fashion, Harty showed audiences the warmth, lyricism and grace. It seems to be in character that he was a marvellous poker player, invariably defeating another great musical exponent of the game, the pianist Moiseiwitsch. The best example of his wit was his remark about the declining fortunes of the British National Opera Company: 'Opera in this country is dying – of T.B.' Beecham himself said nothing better.

Sadly, Harty's relationship with the Hallé committee slowly deteriorated. He had always taken a keen interest in the administration of the concerts, especially after the installation of his mistress, Olive Baguley, as secretary of the Society. The committee were unduly suspicious of his dealings with the Columbia Graphophone Company and increasingly came to feel that their functions were being usurped. Some members of the Society, too, echoed the *Guardian* criticisms of Neville Cardus (who had succeeded Langford in 1927), when he wrote: 'Why do we get, more often than not, the second-rate things in modern music at the Hallé Concerts nowadays?' Cardus was priggishly hostile to the inclusion of Gershwin's *An American in Paris* and this led to a guarantor's statement that 'We don't want your American jazz . . . A lot of stuff he [Harty] puts on is rot'. Harty also displeased the committee by his increasing absences to be guest conductor of the Chicago Symphony Orchestra and by accepting in 1932 the conductorship of the London Symphony Orchestra (cancelling his London concerts with the Hallé at the same time). This, combined with some financial matters, was too much for the committee, who decided not to renew his contract at the end of the 1932-3 season. Harty forestalled announcement of his dismissal by announcing his resignation. In his farewell speech to the regular Hallé subscribers, he made no reference to the controversy surrounding his departure but paid special tribute to his players – 'the most valuable friends I have ever had. It almost seems to me sometimes as though they were prepared to give the very soul out of their bodies if necessary. In fact, when they are playing great music, I think that is what they really do.'

A journalist who interviewed Harty for the *Daily Express* in 1931 described him as an enigma: 'He lives a lonely life in a house in Eccles. He shuns publicity, he affects the utmost fastidiousness in his way of life. He is an utterly charming man to meet, yet one can never be sure what subtle thoughts are lurking behind that bland expansive smile. A great musician, and a fascinatingly, bafflingly complex man.'

Unfortunately his engagement with the L.S.O. did not prove happy. Accustomed to autonomy at the Hallé, he could not accommodate himself to the L.S.O.'s self-governing constitution which enabled the orchestra to engage deputies. This system he regarded (rightly) as inimical to high standards. So his contract was terminated at the end of 1934, just after he had conducted the first performance of the incomplete version of the symphony which Walton had always promised to him. A year later he conducted the completed work, with its finale added, with the B.B.C. Symphony Orchestra. In 1936 his health began to fail and in 1937 it was found that there was a deep-seated malignant growth in his brain. He had to have his right eye removed and did not again conduct in public until a B.B.C. symphony concert on 1 March 1939. He returned to Lancashire – but only to Liverpool – in November of that year, but the remorseless nature of his illness meant fewer engagements. He conducted the B.B.C. Symphony Orchestra at Tunbridge Wells on 1 December 1940. On 19 February 1941 he died, aged sixty-one. Perhaps the most eloquent tribute to this great conductor – and the one he himself would most have cherished – was that paid by an ex-Hallé player, Archie Camden, in 1959: 'When some of us meet,' he said, 'we're apt to talk of the works that haven't been played properly since he died.'

v—Interregnum

Before leaving the Harty era, some significant events in that period should be chronicled. In the summer of 1924 Gustav Behrens resigned the chairmanship at the age of seventy-eight. When a youth of nineteen, working in the Manchester branch of the family shipping-house, he had met Charles Hallé who visited the offices regularly with cheques for his mother to be sent to Hagen. From their talks about music a friendship developed. After Gustav's marriage, Hallé was a frequent guest at the Behrens' home, Holly Royde, in Withington, taking part in musical evenings with some of the most famous musicians of the day. It was Behrens who effectively founded the Hallé Concerts Society. He was on the executive committee from the start, in 1899, and became chairman in 1913. He never sought to hold public office, preferring to serve on committees and to exercise his influence in quiet ways. When he died in 1936 at the age of ninety, the *Manchester Guardian* wrote of him that 'no man did more than he to add "sweetness and light" (the phrase of that distant epoch) to the rather grim philosophy which governed Manchester's development. He was an example of the good European.' One of his last acts as Hallé chairman was to approve the institution of a gold medal to be awarded to members of the orchestra with twenty years' continuous service. The first sixteen recipients were given their medals on 16 October 1924.

In 1925 Arthur Catterall resigned the orchestra's leadership which he had held since 1913. Born in 1883, he was admitted to the Royal Manchester College of Music at the age of ten as a pupil first of Willy Hess, then of Brodsky. He played in the Bayreuth Festival Orchestra in 1902 and was soloist in Tchaikovsky's concerto at a Hallé concert in Manchester, conducted by Richter, on 15 December 1904. For several years he led Henry Wood's Queen's Hall Orchestra before becoming Hallé leader in Balling's time. His relationship with Harty became increasingly prickly. For one thing, he was critical of Harty's interpretations of Beethoven and, for another, they quarrelled when a series of chamber concerts which they founded in 1923 failed after one season and Harty set up a new series (which also failed) in rivalry to the Catterall Quartet. Harty became vindictive and on one occasion, when Catterall was soloist with the Hallé at a concert outside Manchester, made no effort to provide a helpful accompaniment. He was prone to this kind of 'blow hot, blow cold' attitude to people; Neville Cardus has related how one day Harty would be friendly to him and on another, perhaps after a piece of hostile criticism, would ostentatiously 'cut him dead' in a restaurant. John Bridge succeeded Catterall as leader and was himself succeeded by Alfred Barker in 1927.

After the Hallé–Harty 'divorce' in 1933, neither partner in what had been an outwardly successful if privately tempestuous marriage prospered as they might have expected. We have seen the sad decline in Harty's fortunes; his orchestra, too, entered a decade of choppy waters. This was a time of economic depression, large-scale unemployment and international uncertainty. It is significant that after Harty's departure Gustav Behrens, at the age of eighty-six, became honorary treasurer of the society. With Harty had gone Olive Baguley, the secretary; and also vanished were the society's correspondence and records. Behrens straightened out the mess (largely from his own pocket) and appointed R. B. Hesselgrave as secretary. He also introduced a new guarantee system. Hitherto, members of the society, as guarantors, were liable to be called upon for nothing less than £100. But that kind of munificence was shrinking in scale. It now became possible to be a guarantor for £10, or any multiple of £10, with the assurance that not more than a fifth of the sum guaranteed would be asked for in any one year. But these £10 guarantors were not full members.

The big question was: who would succeed Harty? The committee remained convinced that an orchestra achieved its best results under a permanent conductor, despite the temptation to believe that glamorous guest conductors would have more appeal at the box-office. It had been the Hallé's polish and discipline under Harty in 1928 and the Berlin Philharmonic's under Furtwängler later in the same year which had shaken London and had led to the formation of the B.B.C. Symphony Orchestra in 1929-30 under a permanent conductor, Adrian Boult. When they found the right man, the committee said, he would be appointed. It was not long before Sir Thomas Beecham, who had formed the London Philharmonic Orchestra with spectacular success in 1932, was proposing himself, if not as conductor, at least as artistic adviser. The history of Beecham's relationship with the Hallé over the years is nothing if not lively and, sometimes, farcical. It would be approachable entirely as comedy were it not that money was involved and that most organisations which dealt with Beecham, though he could be generous in some respects, found that his financial recklessness and his unreliability took them on to the rocks. He had been a leading light in the plans to form the B.B.C. Symphony Orchestra but, when it came to the point, the B.B.C. disengaged themselves.[1] Now, when he approached the Society with a scheme to obtain eighty Hallé engagements outside Manchester (where twenty-one a season were given) and to obtain conductors and soloists, in conjunction with concert agencies, at reduced rates, the Hallé first showed interest and then refused to become embroiled. It approached Bruno Walter about the conductorship, but his commitments in the United States would not allow him to accept.

Meanwhile the Hallé had come to an arrangement with the B.B.C. As related in the previous chapter, there had been deep resentment over the formation of the B.B.C. Symphony Orchestra, Harty having been particularly incensed by the defection of his superb oboist Alec Whittaker. But, before that, the Corporation had formed a 'Northern Wireless Orchestra', which comprised Hallé players. In 1931 this was disbanded and replaced by a nonet. Seven of its players were contractually forbidden to play with the Hallé outside Manchester and thus were compelled to resign from the Hallé. After a year or so, this was again expanded into the Northern Studio Orchestra. In 1933 this orchestra was augmented by twenty-two Hallé players for thirty

[1]See *The B.B.C. Symphony Orchestra 1930-1980* by Nicholas Kenyon (London, 1981).

broadcast concerts, and in 1934 it became the B.B.C. Northern Orchestra. All its members were Hallé players and they were offered employment all the year round. The Hallé was to be free to use the players in all its engagements and for the eleven concerts a season given for the Liverpool Philharmonic Society. The principal benefit of this arrangement was that the players were kept in regular employment at a time when the Hallé alone could not guarantee sufficient work.

In the 1933-4 season, the first without Harty, Beecham conducted several concerts. The other guest conductors included Robert Heger, Pierre Monteux, Albert Coates, Leslie Heward, Adrian Boult, Nicolai Malko, Sir Edward Bairstow, Sir Henry Wood and John Barbirolli. The last-named, aged thirty-three and recently appointed conductor of the Scottish Orchestra, had first conducted the Hallé during one of Harty's absences in America, on 12 January 1933 when his interpretation of Franck's Symphony had won high praise from Granville Hill in the *Manchester Guardian*. On 15 February 1934 he substituted for Elgar (by then on his deathbed and with only eight days to live) in the Free Trade Hall, conducting an Elgar programme which included the Violin Concerto, with Albert Sammons as soloist, and the *Enigma Variations*. A week later Igor Stravinsky conducted a concert of his own works including the Violin Concerto (soloist Samuel Dushkin), *Fireworks*, the *Suite Italienne* and the *Pastorale* for violin and wind quartet. Stravinsky was not then generally regarded in England as one of the giant figures of twentieth-century music and there were many empty seats. Cardus wrote that 'he will go down to posterity, as far as Manchester is concerned, as a maker of beautiful music, of sweet concourse of sounds'. On 3 March 1934 Egon Petri, who had been professor of the piano at the Royal Manchester College of Music from 1905 to 1910, was soloist in Busoni's Piano Concerto, which was conducted by Brodsky's successor as Principal of the college, R. J. Forbes, himself a fine pianist. On the whole it had been an attractive and fairly enterprising season, but audiences were falling away, particularly for choral concerts. It had been the tradition to perform Handel's *Messiah* on successive evenings before Christmas, but after 1933 this was reduced to one performance. A performance of Verdi's *Requiem* conducted by Sir Henry Wood was given in a Free Trade Hall barely half filled, to the disgust of the conductor (publicly expressed).

Cardus, in his notice of the opening concert of the 1934-5 season, reminded Manchester that a new permanent conductor was needed. 'Perhaps we saw him and heard his work at this concert', he wrote, referring to Georg Szell. He was concerned that, under a system of guest conductors working with one rehearsal for a concert, the quality of programmes would suffer and that there would be no disposition to risk contemporary works. As far as this season was concerned, his fears were justified. Short works by Arnold Cooke, Bax and Delius were played, otherwise the only 'novelty' was on 7 March 1935 when Rachmaninov was solo pianist in the first English performance of his latest work, the *Rhapsody on a Theme of Paganini*, conducted by Malko. Cardus was rather cool about this now popular work but wrote that 'as soon as Rachmaninov walked on to the platform and as soon as we saw his tall, stiff form and his fine, world-weary face we knew we were present at a great concert. Such is genius . . .' Beecham, Barbirolli, Carl Schuricht and Eugen Szenkar were among the guest conductors; and, on 24 January 1935, Malcolm Sargent made his first Hallé appearance when he conducted Bach's Mass in B minor.

Yet perhaps the sensation of the 1934-5 season in Manchester was not a Hallé concert but the first visit on 5 December 1934 by the B.B.C. Symphony Orchestra under Boult. 'The proper place for the B.B.C.'s activities is in the studio', Harty had said in 1930, epitomising the objections from established orchestras to the B.B.C.'s direct competition with them in public concert-halls. This licence-subsidised organisation was regarded by its rivals as engaging in unfair competition. The Hallé committee by 1934 were anxious not to 'rock the boat' with the B.B.C. because of the arrangement with the Northern Orchestra, and E. W. Grommé, chairman of the Society, had given his informal assent to the B.B.C. Symphony Orchestra's visit. But other members of the committee and particularly Forbes, who was now the Society's musical adviser, were hostile to the visit and were supported by the Manchester public, whose loyalty to the Hallé, while admirable, is still an embarrassment where all but a few visiting orchestras are concerned. The orchestra, the *Evening Chronicle* reported, was 'nearly as big as the audience'. Its programme included Hindemith's *Philharmonic Concerto*, Ireland's *Mai-Dun*, Ravel's *Bolero* and Strauss's *Ein Heldenleben* with – irony of ironies in the Hallé headquarters – the violin solos played by the orchestra's leader Arthur Catterall. The critics used up their superlatives to describe the quality of performance and Boult later said they had enjoyed the visit, 'but we were decisively told in many quarters to keep off the Hallé Orchestra's "grass"'. The Hallé's attitude should, of course, be viewed in the context of its economic situation. The deficit on the 1933-4 season had been £611; in 1934-5 it was £383. This was a time when the losses were met by the guarantors, not by municipal or state grants or industrial sponsorship. Moreover engagements were rapidly diminishing. In 1930 the

22

orchestra was giving seventy-five concerts a year; in Harty's last season, 1932-3, this figure had fallen to forty-six. By the end of the 1935-6 season it had dropped to thirty-seven and the Society had only 131 members.

If that looks drab, and if it seems that this was a low ebb in Hallé fortunes, a corrective may be obtained in the columns of the *Manchester Guardian* where Cardus was in full spate during the 1935-6 season. Among the conductors were Beecham, Ernest Ansermet, Vincenzo Bellezza, Sargent and Sir Landon Ronald. The soloists included Vladimir Horowitz and Rachmaninov among the pianists, Bronislaw Huberman among the violinists and Emanuel Feuermann the cellist. If Sibelius's Sixth Symphony was the only unusual 'adventure', there were compensations. Here is Cardus writing after the concert on 16 January 1936: 'The Hallé Concert was the greatest for many years; it received inspiration from Huberman, whose performance of the Brahms Violin Concerto has seldom if ever been matched in this city for intensity. To call it a performance is banal; it was a spiritual experience, a purification, vouchsafed to us by a noble artist . . . Somebody was heard to remark that the tone here and there became thin. And somebody will get to heaven one day and remark that an angel's halo is not on straight . . . The audience knew that a musical experience of no ordinary kind was occurring; seldom have I seen a great crowd so moved and intent . . . The evening also proved that Sir Landon Ronald is still one of the few conductors of our day who can compel an orchestra to sing . . . Because they are different in aesthetic outlook and feeling Sir Landon and Huberman make a satisfactory pair . . . The concerto indeed was heard at its biggest and greatest; maybe it will never be heard again in our lifetime so fully presented . . . Sir Landon Ronald has for years been our best conductor of the music of Elgar . . . He links Elgar the man of action and a rather blatant patriot to Elgar the truer man – the man with the musing eye . . . Sir Landon treated the motto-theme, which begins the [First] Symphony, with a simple gravity that disguised the touch of the commonplace . . . The beautiful slow movement had a solemn mazefulness; the composer turns his mind inward; the vaulted melodies and the dying fall bring us at last to a peacefulness which will always recall a mellow afternoon in Worcester Cathedral.'

A month later, on 27 February 1936, Horowitz played two piano concertos, Tchaikovsky's No. 1 in B flat minor and Brahms's No. 1 in D minor. Cardus wrote: 'The playing in the Tchaikovsky concerto was exquisite – a strange way, you might think, of treating a hackneyed battle-scarred work that usually has been hammered by the pugilists of the keyboard into cast-iron vulgarity. But the truth is that there are passages in the music of rapid figuration so delicate that, swiftly, lightly and delicately performed as they were by Horowitz, they seem born of the purest fantasy . . . They were spun into the air for no other reason than to please us, and we could but love their gossamer irrelevances. Cascades of notes fell from the heights to the depths of the keyboard, and the orchestra tried in vain to match the pianist's ravishments . . . Horowitz is deepening in expression – musical expression – every day. His Brahms at this concert was not Teuton, but by no means small. There was eloquence without effect, and without the obvious classical attitude . . . Dr Sargent in both concertos directed the orchestra watchfully, and hardly anything went wrong.'

Earlier in this winter, Manchester (on 4 December 1935) heard Furtwängler's Berlin Philharmonic at a Brand Lane concert. Cardus described the scene at the end as recalling 'a revivalist meeting' in its fervour. They played Haydn's 'Surprise' Symphony (No. 94), Brahms's First Symphony and Stravinsky's *Firebird* suite. 'Has Manchester, or anywhere else, heard a more breathtaking tour de force of orchestral technique than the performance of Stravinsky's *Firebird* suite?' Cardus asked. 'The colour, verve, precision, and the unfailing instinct for beauty – nothing could have been more remarkable or ravishing.' The Haydn Cardus found 'manly and firm – and a little unsmiling', the Brahms was 'titanic'. As for the orchestra, 'again we were impressed by the symphonic roundness of tone, the richness of texture which no English orchestra seems able to obtain . . . There is style and technical mastery in every department; best of all, there is idealism and high-mindedness.'

'Another enormous audience' was at the Hallé Concert on 12 March 1936 to hear Rachmaninov play his own D minor concerto (No. 3). 'He does not come to music via the piano,' Cardus wrote, 'but to the piano via musical sensibility. In other words, he plays from the creative centre outwards – not from the piano inwards . . . We were taken into the artist's workshop – I had almost written "forge", but that would have flattered the value, as powerful music, of the D minor concerto. It is a fine composition of its kind, much subtler in its figuration than the better-known second concerto. But it rings the changes on, and adds nothing to, the familiar Rachmaninov formulae . . . None of the foreign conductors who have visited us recently has accompanied a concerto with Mr Forbes's understanding and experienced perception. Rachmaninov obviously was always at ease . . . He keeps us always fascinated because there is, no matter how many times he comes before us, an enigma about his art. His power, lyricism, brilliance are

Hans Richter and Sir Hamilton Harty

Four popular Hallé conductors: (*above*) Michael Balling (Henry Watson Music Library/City of Manchester Cultural Services); Sir Thomas Beecham; (*below*) Sir Malcolm Sargent (both *Daily Telegraph*); Arvid Yansons

somehow masked or withdrawn; we cannot really share in them; we must remain at a distance.'

Beecham ended the season on 16 March with Brahms's Second Symphony and Berlioz's *Symphonie Fantastique*. The latter, Cardus said, was played 'with verve, imagination and considerable technical skill. Sir Thomas's conducting was as brilliant and audacious and as red hot with genius as any he has given us this season, or ever.' Cardus congratulated the orchestra on 'a season of good hard work . . . The Hallé Concerts Society has had a wide experience now of conductors in the limited class which is within Manchester's power of attraction – and within the Society's spending powers. The policy of the future seems plain enough now; a more or less permanent man to take charge and attend to technical points week by week, so that the orchestra can always be trusted to respond at once to the promptings of great virtuosi conductors such as Sir Thomas.' Perhaps Cardus had heard what was in the wind: that Gustav Behrens's son Leonard, who had joined the committee in 1932, had in December 1935 come out strongly in favour of appointing Sargent as conductor, while doing nothing to break 'the invaluable bond with Beecham'. It was decided to defer the matter for a year.

Pierre Monteux conducted the first two concerts of the 1936-7 season, with Rubinstein playing Brahms's B flat Piano Concerto on 15 October. Wood's two concerts included Glazunov's Sixth Symphony and Vaughan Williams's *A Sea Symphony*. Ronald conducted Rachmaninov's Second Symphony and Elgar's Violin Concerto (Henry Holst). Constant Lambert conducted Sibelius's Second Symphony on 26 November; and on 4 February 1937, Barbirolli, having just completed his first ten weeks as conductor of the New York Philharmonic-Symphony Orchestra in succession to Toscanini, conducted his first Hallé performance of Elgar's Second Symphony. The majority of concerts were divided between Sargent and Beecham. Sargent's *Messiah* soloists make nostalgic reading – Isobel Baillie, Muriel Brunskill, Webster Booth, Harold Williams – and he also conducted Palestrina's *Stabat Mater*, Berlioz's *L'Enfance du Christ*, Bax's Fourth, Sibelius's Third, Brahms's Fourth and Schubert's Ninth Symphonies, a Beethoven evening with Huberman soloist in the Violin Concerto, and the Rachmaninov *Rhapsody on a Theme of Paganini* with Moiseiwitsch solo pianist. Beecham kept to familiar ground except for Berners's *Triumph of Neptune*, Walton's *Façade* Suite No. 1 and Vaughan Williams's *Norfolk Rhapsody*. He conducted Brahms's First and Third Symphonies, Sibelius's First, Beethoven's Third and Seventh, some Mozart and

25

Haydn and Dvořák's Cello Concerto with Feuermann. The profit on the season was £707.

In 1937-8 the profit was £523. Sargent conducted eleven of the concerts. His programmes included Delius's *Song of the High Hills*, Debussy's *Nocturnes* and Holst's *The Planets*, all employing the choir wordlessly, and the first Manchester performance (on 24 February 1938) of Walton's First Symphony which Cardus thought 'an impressionist reading rather than an exact account'. Beecham's seven concerts included Delius's *Sea-Drift* and the Sixth and Seventh Symphonies of Sibelius.

The season occasioned some caustic comment at the annual general meeting in 1937 from a new member of the committee, Philip Godlee, chairman of Simpson and Godlee, textile manufacturers, and himself a talented amateur musician. He spoke of the perennial difficulty of combining progressive programmes with box-office success. The 'meagre audience' for the Walton symphony – the Hallé's 'one great effort' in 1937-8 – had disturbed him. He also urged a reduction in the size of the choir and the abandonment by its women members of their 'white raiment', and called on the City Council to modernise the Free Trade Hall by providing comfortable seats, as in cinemas, and air-conditioning.

Throughout these years the puckish spirit of Beecham enlivened the proceedings. He had at one point decided that it was time Manchester heard Stravinsky's *Rite of Spring*. But the parts went astray or were too expensive and the idea was dropped. He suggested a Beethoven symphony in its place. No, there had been too much Beethoven, what about Mendelssohn's 'Italian' Symphony? Impossible, said Beecham, on only two rehearsals. It was pointed out to him that he had been prepared to do the Stravinsky on two rehearsals. 'Quite so', he replied, 'I could play the "Rite" well enough on two rehearsals. For the 'Italian' Symphony five at least are necessary.' Rehearsing Strauss's *Ein Heldenleben* he sent the trumpeters off-stage for the beginning of the battle section. As they went towards the exit, he called out, 'You will come back, won't you?' On another foggy morning in the Free Trade Hall he opened the rehearsal with: 'We'll play Delius's *In a Summer Garden*, very suitable for the occasion.' When Philip Godlee asked him what one of his particularly extravagant gestures to the orchestra meant, he replied: 'It means I don't know where the devil we've got to.' Beecham, like Harty, could wince under Cardus's criticisms, though he and Cardus were good friends. In September 1937, Beecham wrote to the Hallé committee to say that he would 'refuse to conduct any concert to which Mr Neville Cardus is invited'. The committee correctly replied to the effect that they invited the *Guardian* and it was up to the *Guardian* which critic they sent.

Having survived the 1937-8 season, Cardus was still in his *Guardian* seat for the opening of the 1938-9 season by Beecham on 20 October. 'Man and boy we have all been going to the Hallé concerts these many years,' he began, 'and man and boy we have all been listening to the same music . . . The playing throughout this concert promised excellent work to come as soon as the instrumentalists have got together again. It is the tragedy of the Hallé Orchestra that only for half the year can we proudly call it a permanent combination; by the time March is reached the Hallé Orchestra has no superior in the land for strength and grasp of symphonic musical shape. Then the forces are disbanded to the four winds, or to as many winds as blow across our various seaside piers. The performance of Tchaikovsky's *Francesca da Rimini* was evidence in itself of the quickness of the Hallé players to pick up their resources from the place where every spring they are compelled to lay them down . . . Sir Thomas directed the whirlwind consummately; his gestures were even more drastic than ever before. On one occasion he achieved the best square-cut I have seen since Macartney retired. But he should try to get nearer to the ball and over it, while making his leg-glance.' Obviously they were friends again.

At the concert on 1 December 1938, Arthur Bliss conducted his *Checkmate* ballet and the rest of the programme was in the charge of Constant Lambert, who had Petri as soloist in piano concertos by Mozart (No. 23 in A, K. 488) and Liszt. Cardus thought the Mozart occasionally lacked graciousness, but in the Liszt A major concerto 'Mr Petri again let us understand that he is one of the few royalist pianists of the present age; nobody living plays Liszt better . . . It was refreshing to hear the instrument played in the grand manner once more . . . Mr Lambert controlled the orchestral part firmly and freely . . . Here is another conductor who would be a godsend to the Hallé Orchestra if he were put in charge.' A fortnight later, Schnabel played two piano concertos: Brahms's No. 1 in D minor and Beethoven's No. 1 in C. 'At the end of the slow movement of the Brahms concerto,' Cardus reported, 'there was that great release of breath, that wide stirring upon the surface of consciousness which tells that men and women have for a while been lost to this world and all its silly, shabby troubles . . . Schnabel has been known to devour his conductor. But . . . he is capable of simple and sublime yieldings, given a conductor whose control is not narrow or a sign of impotence. Dr Sargent knows Schnabel well; the Hallé Orchestra knows him well . . . The only thing wanting in the Brahms concerto was that ideal shading of orchestral tone which none of us will ever forget who heard Sir Hamilton Harty conduct the work.'

On 2 February 1939 Felix Weingartner, in his seventy-sixth year, conducted the Hallé in a Brahms programme containing the First and Third Symphonies. Cardus reminded his readers that they had encountered a piece of musical history: 'When he was twenty he went to see Liszt, and he took with him an opera of his own composition. He was famous in the legendary age of Berlin and Vienna. He knew Brahms. And here he was, holding us in his hand on a cold night in Manchester.' The Hallé players 'had many chances to dwell lovingly on choice moments and to inflect eloquently'. Weingartner, he summed up, 'belongs to the cultured epoch of music, the epoch of good manners and good taste – and sound scholarship'. At the concert a week later, Sargent conducted Elgar's *The Dream of Gerontius*, with Gladys Ripley, Heddle Nash and Harold Williams. 'An older Elgarian than myself', Cardus wrote, 'assured me that he has never heard a better performance, and he has been present at most of them since the festival at Düsseldorf [in 1902] . . . Dr Sargent has done nothing more compelling than this . . . [He] achieved an ideal balance between choir and soloists, there was no hint of strain, little forcing of effects beyond the ends intended by Elgar.'

Huberman returned on 16 February again to play the Brahms Violin Concerto, with Sargent conducting, and Cardus found that 'the wonderful experience of a year or two ago . . . was not repeated . . . Maybe the ordinary ear craved now and again for a more palpable romanticism of expression and a richer tone'. This programme also contained the first Hallé performance of Moeran's Symphony in G minor. 'Sibelius's taciturnity is the one thing which his followers seem unwilling to emulate in their master,' Cardus remarked. '. . . As a symphony the work failed for want of contrast of material; a symphony should not diminish into a soliloquy.' Modern British music was never Cardus's strong point. On 23 February Emanuel Feuermann's playing of Dvořák's Cello Concerto was 'some of the richest cello-playing heard in Manchester for years'. Sargent then conducted Elgar's *Falstaff* which Cardus believed was 'never likely to become a general favourite' because of its subtlety. 'Dr Sargent and the Hallé Orchestra emphasised the realism at some expense of the contemplative parts,' but 'all in all, the interpretation satisfied us once again that Dr Sargent is a true Elgarian.' There was more English music, from Beecham, on 2 March. In Delius's *Appalachia*, 'the playing of the orchestra left far behind anything achieved this season. It is astounding how Sir Thomas, on the strength of one short stay in the city, can transform good craftsmen into eloquent and even poetic artists.' On 9 March, Rachmaninov returned to play his C minor concerto. As usual, Cardus reported, he 'wore the air of a weary man; he toiled towards the piano, bowed inscrutably, seemed to conceal a sigh of resigned boredom, then began to bewitch us, and possibly himself, by playing that seemed to awaken from his instrument all the music it has known and heard during a long epoch in which great pianists have wooed it, cultivated it and taught it the language of romance. Rachmaninov is the most comprehensive of his craft...' Cardus wondered how, in Sargent's hands, music as familiar as Brahms's Fourth Symphony 'could possibly be made to sound so strange'. Sargent 'almost caused the E minor of Brahms to remind us of the E minor of Tchaikovsky's Fifth. Brahms calls for the elegiac note in this first movement, which received a contemporary dynamic effectiveness... Dr Sargent is less a reflective than an active conductor; he seems to live in the present and to feel music as a succession of episodes...'

It is doubtful, therefore, if Cardus supported Sargent as a contender for the conductorship of the Hallé. In January 1939 Philip Godlee stressed to the committee the urgency of an appointment. He mentioned Goossens and Lambert but thought that Sargent had 'many irons in the fire and I doubt whether Manchester would ever be his chief interest'. (Sargent conducted many choral societies and was involved with the London Philharmonic in its Courtauld–Sargent concerts.) Godlee put the case for a permanent conductor who would eliminate the prevailing 'haphazard' system of choosing programmes and increase the number of concerts. 'When was there last a musical "event" at a Hallé Concert?' he asked. 'When was a London critic last present? Not since Harty's time.' Godlee was prescient, for when Grommé and Leonard Behrens approached Sargent in February, Sargent objected to the term 'permanent conductor', saying that he could not accept that the Hallé should be his principal interest and he would not live in Manchester. But he promised he would not subordinate his interest in the Hallé to any other concerts. Forbes was violently opposed to this compromise, but in April 1939 it was announced that Sargent would be 'conductor-in-chief and musical adviser' until 1940-1, although he would not be available for the first two concerts of the 1939-40 season because he would be in Australia. The Hallé plan was to offer these two concerts to Harty, but, alas, this reconciliation never occurred. Another change occurred in the leadership, Laurance Turner taking over from Barker. Thus matters stood on 3 September 1939 when the Second World War began. Yes, the concerts had declined in status since Harty's departure, but what would we not give today to be hearing soloists like Rachmaninov, Schnabel, Horowitz, Feuermann and Huberman?

VI—*Godlee's decision*

As Gustav Behrens had decided twenty-five years earlier that war should not halt the Hallé Concerts, so E. W. Grommé decided again in 1939. But this time the Society had to find a new home because the Free Trade Hall was taken over as a store. In place of the weekly Thursday concerts, it was decided to give ten Sunday afternoon concerts in the Paramount (now Odeon) Cinema in Oxford Street, Manchester. Beecham conducted the first, on 22 October 1939. Wood and Sargent were the other conductors. Although no one could know it then, when Beecham ended the concert on 3 December with a glorious performance of Strauss's *Morning, Noon and Night in Vienna* he had conducted the Hallé for the last time. In May 1940 he went to the United States and on his return in 1944 – well, we shall see what happened then. Also in 1940 Neville Cardus departed to Australia. These two luminaries were never again to shine together in the Hallé constellation. Wood conducted the first Manchester performance of Vaughan Williams's *A London Symphony* (twenty-six years after its first performance!) and Sargent introduced the music of Edmund Rubbra to the concerts with the Third Symphony. He also conducted Delius's *Sea-Drift* and the first Hallé performance of Bliss's *Morning Heroes*, with John Gielgud as narrator. For the 1940-1 season, a grim winter of blitz following the expectation of summer invasion, the number of concerts was doubled to twenty, the principal composers represented being Wagner, Beethoven, Brahms, Tchaikovsky, Elgar, Sibelius and Debussy. Among the soloists were the soprano Eva Turner, the violinists Ida Haendel, Eda Kersey and Laurance Turner, the pianists Pouishnoff, Cyril Smith, Moiseiwitsch, Eileen Joyce, R. J. Forbes and Lucy Pierce, the cellist Haydn Rogerson (the Hallé principal), and Archie Camden, the bassoonist. Nearly twenty members of the orchestra were now in the Services, but among the familiar names still playing were Reginald Stead, Philip Hecht, Arthur Percival and Don Hyden (violins), Frank Park (viola), Arthur Shaw (double bass), Joe Lingard (flute), Pat Ryan (clarinet), Otto Paersch (horn), Arthur Lockwood (trumpet), the trombone team Holt, Old and Hoyland, Wallace Jones (tuba), Jack Massey (timpani) and Charles Collier (harp).

The summer of 1940 had seen the evacuation of Dunkirk and the beginning of the 'Battle of Britain', momentous events. Yet even in such a crisis, the arts had not been neglected, the Government perhaps having been surprised by the immense upsurge of public interest in theatre, music, literature and painting. The Council for the Encouragement of Music and the Arts, forerunner of the Arts Council, was established and gave money from the exchequer for concerts, plays and similar events. R. J. Forbes did not exaggerate at the 1940 Hallé annual meeting when he described this subsidy as 'the most striking thing which has occurred in the history of music in England . . . We hope this will not be a wartime measure but that it will mark a new era in music'. The Hallé's share of this bounty was £1,000 for eleven concerts in the autumn of 1940 in various industrial towns.

These concerts, more of which followed, were administered by the anti-Sargent Forbes, who regarded the Hallé as under obligation to Sargent only for the Manchester series. There was trouble for Sargent, too, from the orchestra. They regarded him as their chief conductor and protested to the committee when he appeared in Manchester and other towns with the London Philharmonic. These objections were taken up with Sargent by the committee, who accepted his explanation, and he was eventually confirmed as conductor for the 1941-2 season, with fourteen out of the twenty Manchester concerts. This season was given in the Opera House, Quay Street, where six concerts conducted by Sir Adrian Boult had been given in April 1941, followed by twelve promenade concerts in May, ten of which were conducted by Sargent and two by Boult. The Free Trade Hall had been a casualty of the fire blitz on Manchester on the night of 22 December 1940, when only its outer façade was left standing. This, of course, had no effect on the Hallé, but the city council's decision to allow Sunday opening of cinemas had deprived the Society of the Paramount. The 1941-2 season included the first Manchester performance (by Henry Holst) of Walton's Violin Concerto, Elgar's Violin Concerto (Albert Sammons) and Second Symphony, Delius's *In a Summer Garden*, six major works by Sibelius, Dvořák's Violin Concerto and *Symphonic Variations* and, in memory of a great Hallé conductor, Harty's *Ode to a Nightingale*. The conductors besides Sargent were Boult and Leslie Heward.

All this time the arrangement with the B.B.C. Northern Orchestra continued. It had always been irksome – arguments over rehearsal fees, joint negotiations on promotions within the ranks of the two orchestras, and interpretation of Musicians' Union agreements – but as the war continued and the public's appetite for music grew, it became a severe brake on Hallé expansion. The Hallé was compelled to refuse engagements because it could not be sure until five weeks before the date of any concert that its thirty-five joint Hallé–B.B.C. players would be available. A loss of £705 on the 1939-40 season and £870 in 1940-1 meant that it was essential for the orchestra to give more concerts. The B.B.C., through Maurice Johnstone, were not unsympathetic and in the summer of 1941 a twelve-month scheme was devised whereby the B.B.C. players were released to the Hallé for thirty three-day weekends. For the twenty-two weeks May to September the B.B.C. players stayed on their twenty-hour-per-week contract, with occasional Hallé concerts. For the thirty weeks October to April the twenty-hour contract would lapse and studio concerts be reduced from five a week to three. This arrangement ran through the 1941-2 season, on which a profit of over £1,500 on ninety-three concerts was made.

Philip Godlee was emerging as the principal figure in Hallé affairs because of his chairmanship of the music sub-committee. Tall, with an artificial leg, an artificial eye and a body full of shrapnel as mementoes of the First World War, he was yet a strikingly handsome figure. He had a saturnine charm, devastating wit, and a buccaneering enjoyment in taking risks. He could make swift, autocratic decisions or mastermind a strategy of cunning inactivity. Impatient of fools and of bureaucracy, he could control a committee by subtle removal and replacement of his monocle. He was a man of courage and of compassion. For the 1942-3 season, Sargent was offered fourteen concerts, although it had been intended that he should have only six concerts while Leslie Heward would be offered at least twelve, with a view to Heward's being appointed permanent conductor for 1943-4. Unfortunately, Heward was already a sick man and unable to take on so much work. Because the Opera House management refused to continue to let the theatre for concerts, the Hallé had to find new venues for the twenty-four Sunday concerts. Eventually twelve were given at the Longford Cinema, Stretford (later the Essoldo and now the Ladbroke Social Club), eight at the Capitol Cinema, Didsbury (now a television studio), three in Manchester Hippodrome, and *Messiah* in the King's Hall in Belle Vue entertainment park. But before this Manchester season opened, the Hallé in 1942 had the busiest summer of its history, playing to forty thousand people in three weeks in May. In June it visited London for the first time since Harty had left.

Works performed during the 1942-3 Manchester season included Bliss's *Music for Strings*, Elgar's First Symphony and Cello Concerto, Scriabin's Piano Concerto, Shostakovich's First Symphony and the first Hallé performance of music by Benjamin Britten, his *Sinfonia da Requiem* which Basil Cameron conducted on 24 January 1943. On 28 February, at Stretford, Leslie Heward conducted Beethoven's 'Eroica' Symphony. The *marcia funebre* was to be sadly prophetic. A few weeks later he was dead. During the 1942-3 season, the orchestra had given the highest number of concerts in its history (144), and the profit was £224.

Early in 1942 the Hallé committee heard of an important development in Liverpool, where the corporation bought (for £35,000) the modern Philharmonic Hall, which had been opened only in June 1939 and had survived the air raids. The corporation agreed to pay the Philharmonic Society an annuity of £4,000 and to grant free use of the hall to the Society provided that a certain number of concerts was given, and that a permanent orchestra was maintained. Hitherto, for over a century, Liverpool's orchestra had largely comprised Hallé players. Now the Society was able to form an autonomous orchestra – a decision prompted by the sudden disbandment of the B.B.C. Salon Orchestra which had been based in Liverpool and which included such players as David Wise (leader), Léon Goossens (oboe), Anthony Pini (cello) and Reginald Kell (clarinet). These were all engaged for the new Liverpool Philharmonic Orchestra and Sargent was appointed principal conductor. There was also a recording contract. This was enough for Godlee. When the first year of the revised B.B.C.-Hallé arrangement expired in July, he met the B.B.C. representatives, pleaded for the B.B.C. Northern members to be released to the Hallé on one other day each week, and was told the matter would be considered. Five months later, the Hallé committee had a letter from Herbert Dakin, secretary of Sheffield Philharmonic Society, proposing that the Hallé should become a full-time salaried orchestra, giving at least one hundred and fifty concerts a year, maintained by Manchester, Sheffield, Leeds, Bradford and the B.B.C. Municipal subsidy should also be sought.

On 30 December 1942 Godlee became Hallé chairman in succession to P. M. Oliver. Within a month he had agreed in principle to Sheffield's plan. Then, in February 1943, came an offer to the Hallé to take part in a national series of summer concerts; if it was unable to do so, then the Manchester concerts would be provided by the Liverpool Philharmonic or a London orchestra. The B.B.C. told the Hallé that the B.B.C. Northern members would not be available to the Hallé from 19 June to 5 September except on one day. Godlee's mind was now made up to 'go it alone'. He had recently been reminded by the Hallé leader, Laurance Turner, what a fine conductor John Barbirolli was.

Turner had heard that Barbirolli, who had been almost lost to music in Britain since 1936 when he succeeded Toscanini as conductor of the New York Philharmonic, was anxious to return to Britain. Godlee did not know him, but R. J. Forbes did. So, without consulting anyone else on the committee, Godlee authorised the sending of an historic telegram to the United States on 25 February 1943: 'Would you be interested permanent conductorship Hallé? Important developments pending. Robert Forbes. Royal College of Music Manchester.'

VII—*Barbirolli*

John (Giovanni Battista) Barbirolli was a Cockney, born in Holborn on 2 December 1899, of Italian and French parentage. He was short in stature, dynamic in personality. His father and grandfather were violinists and had settled in England in 1892. Lorenzo, Barbirolli's father, played in theatre orchestras and eventually conducted a small orchestra at the Queen's Hotel, Leicester Square. The child Giovanni began to play the cello when he was seven and at the age of ten entered Trinity College of Music, transferring to the Royal Academy of Music in 1912. In 1916 he became the youngest member of Henry Wood's Queen's Hall Orchestra and in 1917 gave his first solo recital in London. After a short spell in the Army, during which he had his first experience as a conductor, he returned to civilian life in 1919, playing in orchestras and bands in dance-halls, hotels, cinemas and circuses as well as in Beecham's orchestra at Covent Garden, in the London Symphony Orchestra, and in the orchestra for Diaghilev's Russian Ballet. He also appeared as solo cellist in Elgar's concerto with the Bournemouth Municipal Orchestra in 1921. Early in 1924 Barbirolli became cellist in two string quartets. But conducting was his ambition and later that year he formed his own chamber orchestra, giving enterprising concerts in London. Frederic Austin, artistic director of the British National Opera Company, was sufficiently impressed by him in December 1925 to offer him engagements with the company. Barbirolli made his operatic début in Gounod's *Roméo et Juliette* in Newcastle upon Tyne in September 1926. Within three months he was attracting critical praise, of which this from the *Birmingham Post* was typical and prescient: 'What is certain is that the soul of music is in him.' He first conducted in Manchester on 17 November 1926 when The B.N.O.C. performed Puccini's *Madama Butterfly*. In 1927 he conducted the London Symphony Orchestra, signed a recording contract with H.M.V. and in 1928 conducted opera at Covent Garden. In 1930 he became conductor of Covent Garden's touring company until its demise in 1933, when he was appointed conductor of the Scottish Orchestra in Glasgow. During these years he made several concerto recordings with Rubinstein, Kreisler, Heifetz and other international artists. Their assessment of him was in contrast to that of the English musical establishment, which still regarded him as 'promising' and was taken aback in 1936 when the New York Philharmonic invited him to succeed Arturo Toscanini as its permanent conductor. Thus at thirty-six he found himself with one of the toughest orchestral assignments in the world, for the N.Y.P.O. of that era was nicknamed 'Murder Incorporated' because of its harsh treatment of some conductors. As it happened, the orchestra respected and eventually loved the young Englishman; after three years his contract was renewed. Where he encountered hostility in New York was from certain critics and from some of the public. The reasons are complex. He was in New York at a time of strong anti-British feeling, when American isolationism from Europe was at its height; in addition, it would not have mattered who followed Toscanini, large sections of the public would have decided he was unworthy. Today, when a more balanced view is taken, it is difficult to realise the extent of the obsession with Toscanini as the ideal conductor. In later years I reminded Barbirolli – who had the added burden from 1938 of seeing Toscanini in charge of rival New York concerts with the N.B.C. Orchestra – that the New York public's Toscanini-mania had made life insupportable for an earlier occupant of the Philharmonic rostrum, none other than Gustav Mahler. Nevertheless, to quote from the entry on Barbirolli in the *New Grove Dictionary of Music and Musicians*, 'to survive there [New York] for five consecutive seasons and to be invited several times to return as guest conductor does not look like failure'. He had many triumphs in New York and he went through a refining fire there. He was far too tough and resilient to have been driven out by hostility, but undoubtedly the experience scarred him for life psychologically and deepened the sense of insecurity which he successfully disguised from all but his closest friends.

The Hallé invitation came at the right moment. Barbirolli's New York contract had not been renewed at the end of the 1941-2 season because of a rule by the American Musicians' Union that after six years any conductor of an American orchestra must become an American citizen. This, especially in wartime, Barbirolli would never have done – despite having no British blood in his veins, he was British through and through. He was desperately worried about his family in

London and, after a brief return visit to England in 1942 as a guest conductor, was determined to return there, even though the Los Angeles Philharmonic was trying to persuade him to stay in the United States. When Forbes's telegram arrived, Barbirolli said to his wife, the oboist Evelyn Rothwell, 'This is it.' He cabled back his interest in the Hallé post.

Encouraged by Barbirolli's response but still saying nothing about it, Godlee called a Hallé committee meeting for 3 March 1943, at which he decided on a show-down with the B.B.C. The Hallé was to be placed immediately on an annual contract. Advertisements appeared in the press inviting applications for posts with the Hallé on the basis of a yearly contract, at least union minimum rate, and two-hundred concerts a year. The committee then awaited the response of the thirty-five B.B.C. Northern players, several of them principals of sections. The B.B.C. offered them thirty-six hours a week instead of twenty at increased rates of pay. They had until 20 March to decide. Writing to Barbirolli on 5 March Forbes had said: 'I don't think there is much doubt that all the Northern players will leave the B.B.C. and come to the Hallé.' In the event, only four of the thirty-five did so. Further, Barbirolli's agent in England was misinformed by the Ministry of Information that Barbirolli was graded for the American Army and could not leave the United States. In a panic, Forbes and Godlee offered the conductorship to Sir Henry Wood, who fortunately refused, because almost the next day Barbirolli cabled to say that he was free to leave. On 5 April Godlee cabled a formal offer of the Hallé post from 1 July at £3,500 a year for 150 concerts. This was increased a week later to £3,750. Barbirolli wrote to Godlee on 18 April: 'I am hoping that you are planning a considerable decentralisation of the concerts, so that one well-rehearsed programme played in Manchester can be played two or three times in nearby districts. Only by constant and detailed rehearsing can an orchestra be led to the heights, and my ambitions for the reconstructed Hallé are high indeed . . . I only hope that your courage and vision will be rewarded as it deserves.'

News of Barbirolli's appointment reached the British public in a newspaper report. The Hallé confirmed it on 19 April. In the middle of a war it did not count as 'big news'. To the average member of the Hallé audience, the dispute with the B.B.C. was a long-running saga; and who was this new conductor? Manchester had not seen him for six or seven years. He was a name on gramophone records. He arrived in Manchester on 2 June 1943, to be met at London Road (now Piccadilly) station by Godlee and Forbes. He then discovered, as he put it semi-humorously years later, that the inducements offered to him in

Forbes's letter were 'almost fraudulent'. After 30 June, when the 'old' Hallé disbanded, he would have an orchestra of thirty-nine players. Forbes had said there would probably be a choice of very good players from other orchestras; this was not so. 'There are sufficient funds available in the form of guarantees to make the venture a sound one,' Forbes had written. Pressed on this, Godlee admitted the funds would last 'about a fortnight – we took a risk!' Barbirolli discovered, too, that the Hallé, under his conductorship, had been booked for a week of concerts from 5 to 10 July at the Prince's Theatre, Bradford, so that he had under five weeks in which to engage thirty players and to weld them and the remaining thirty-nine into an orchestra. But to train an orchestra was what he had come to do, and he exploded with rage when he discovered that at five of the six Bradford concerts a piano concerto was to be played – piano concertos were almost *de rigueur* at wartime concerts. He had not returned to Britain, he said, to be a concerto accompanist. He agreed to retain one of the engaged soloists (Clifford Curzon). So within a few hours, the Hallé committee had learned that its new conductor had a will of his own and a determination to order matters the way he wanted them.

For the next three weeks an intensive series of auditions was held. In London Barbirolli heard students from the principal colleges. In Manchester, in a room in Forsyth's in Deansgate, he heard players from the Manchester colleges, from theatre orchestras and brass bands. Most young people at this time went into one of the three Services, so, Barbirolli said, 'I had to find the "slightly maimed". It didn't matter to me if they had flat feet so long as they had straight fingers.' In this way he discovered players who had had no previous experience of a symphony orchestra: Enid Roper, a Keighley schoolmistress who played the horn; Joyce Aldous, the blonde timpanist; Maisie Ringham, a trombonist from the Royal Manchester College of Music who also played in a Salvation Army band; Oliver Bannister, a sixteen-year-old flautist from the R.M.C.M.; Patricia Stancliffe, oboist. He relished the memory of one applicant, an elderly double-bass player who rarely moved his left hand. To negotiate the leap from C flat to F flat in Act IV of Verdi's *Otello* was a seeming impossibility for him, so Barbirolli took his instrument and played the passage concerned. 'What, oop theer?' the old man exclaimed. 'Oop theer? Ah've never been oop theer before.'

These untried recruits had – luckily for them – to be blended with players of rich and long experience: the leader Laurance Turner, and Philip Hecht, principal second violin; Arthur Shaw, double bass; Haydn Rogerson, Stuart Knussen and Gladys Yates, cellists; Herbert

Mitton, bassoon; Pat Ryan, clarinet; Arthur Lockwood, trumpet; Wallace Jones, tuba; and links with Richter's day, Charles Collier the harpist, and Harry Schofield, double bass. Barbirolli engaged Livia Gollancz (daughter of the publisher Victor Gollancz and later to be managing director of the publishing firm) as principal horn and he brought in Tommy Cheetham, an old friend from the Scottish Orchestra period, as librarian and percussion-player. On Sunday 27 June, Barbirolli was at the Longford, Stretford, to hear the 'old' Hallé give its last concert under Sargent (a memorial programme for Leslie Heward). Next morning he began rehearsals of the 'new' Hallé, his Hallé, at first only about sixty strong. He rehearsed in Houldsworth Hall for nine hours a day, then went home to spend most of the night 'bowing' master copies of string parts. The final rehearsal was open to the press. The *Yorkshire Post* music critic wrote that to create virtually a new orchestra of great quality in wartime could only be regarded as little short of miraculous, 'but there can be no doubt that the miracle has been achieved with the newly formed Hallé Orchestra'. A third of the personnel was female.

The audience for the first Bradford concert on 5 July was not large, but its enthusiasm grew as the evening progressed. Barbirolli's first programme was Wagner's *Meistersinger* overture, Delius's *A Song of Summer*, Tchaikovsky's *Romeo and Juliet* and Brahms's Second Symphony. At the end of the concert he told the audience: 'I have been entrusted with a very great mission – that the name and fame of this great orchestra shall not, under my guidance, achieve less honour in the future than it has done in the past.' Already he saw it as a crusade. By the third concert the theatre was sold out and queues for tickets formed in mid-afternoon. The players were as keen as their conductor. When he arrived at the theatre one morning he 'found the place sounding like a conservatory of music. Entire sections and sub-sections had come down before scheduled rehearsal time and were practising.'

In the subsequent eight weeks Barbirolli took the Hallé to Edinburgh for a week, to Glasgow for a week and to Newcastle upon Tyne, Harrogate, Hanley, Leeds, Halifax and Wolverhampton. It was a triumphal progress, as these extracts from newspaper criticism make plain: 'There is a superb body of violin tone, a powerful brass of fine quality, and the wind band is excellent in every department. It is an orchestra of which Mr Barbirolli has a right to be proud . . . The *Enigma Variations* have the status of a classic, and Mr Barbirolli's rendering of them touched perfection' (*The Scotsman*); 'Of the playing of Brahms's Second Symphony it can only be said that from the rich eloquence of its opening to the sweeping magnificence of its close it was a perfect example of music as conceived by a master mind . . . Not less welcome has been the realisation that in Mr Barbirolli we have one of the greatest conductors of the day' (*Yorkshire Post*). And a writer in the *Observer* said: 'The new Hallé Orchestra promises to set up a new Hallé standard. There are intimations of a rarer refinement than we have hitherto known.' Manchester's first hearing of Barbirolli's Hallé was on 15 August 1943 when six thousand people filled the circus seats in King's Hall, Belle Vue, for the *Meistersinger* overture, Debussy's *L'Après-midi d'un faune*, Elgar's *Enigma Variations* and Tchaikovsky's Fifth Symphony. Granville Hill wrote in the *Manchester Guardian*: 'The orchestral playing was indeed finer than any we have heard in Manchester for many years.'

Barbirolli's first full season (the orchestra's eighty-sixth) began at the Longford, Stretford, on 3 October 1943 with Beethoven's *Egmont* overture. A new (1939) work was introduced to Manchester, Vaughan Williams's *Five Variants on Dives and Lazarus*, and the other two works were the second *Daphnis and Chloë* suite of Ravel and Brahms's Fourth Symphony. This concert was preceded by fourteen rehearsals. Barbirolli's determination to train his orchestra in the standard repertoire is shown by the choice of symphonies: Brahms's First and Second, Beethoven's First, Third, Fifth, Seventh and Eighth, Tchaikovsky's Fourth, Fifth and Sixth, Mendelssohn's 'Italian', Dvořák's Eighth and Ninth, Mozart's 36th and 40th, Haydn's 97th, Sibelius's First and Second, Bizet's and Franck's. Particularly noteworthy was the choice of overtures, Berlioz's *Benvenuto Cellini* and *Carnaval Romain*, Smetana's *The Bartered Bride*, Rossini's *L'Italiana in Algeri* and *Semiramide*, Borodin's *Prince Igor*, Wolf-Ferrari's *The Secret of Susanna*, and Weber's *Euryanthe*. Two of Bach's Brandenburg Concertos (Nos. 3 and 4) were conducted by Barbirolli, as well as Mozart's *Serenata Notturna*. He conducted an operatic programme (Mozart, Gounod, Verdi, Puccini and Wagner) and, at the Capitol, Didsbury, on 13 February 1944, the first of his popular Viennese programmes, ranging from Schubert's Fourth Symphony to Strauss's *Gipsy Baron* overture. He conducted Debussy's *La Mer*, Elgar's Violin Concerto (with Albert Sammons) and *Introduction and Allegro*, Bax's Third Symphony (which he recorded), Brahms's Violin Concerto, a suite from Fauré's *Pelléas et Mélisande*, Ravel's *Mother Goose*, Berlioz's *Symphonie Fantastique* (after which members of the audience stood on their seats yelling 'Bravo'), Sir George Dyson's Symphony, Delius's Double Concerto, and D'Indy's *Symphony on a Mountain Song* (with Kathleen Long as solo pianist). At the Odeon, Prestwich, on

12 December he conducted items from Walton's *Façade* and interrupted the Swiss Yodelling Song to tell the audience that they should laugh, not sit 'like a wall of impenetrable grimness'. He played the jokes again and they laughed. There were piano concertos, too: Moiseiwitsch soloist in Rachmaninov's D minor, Kathleen Long in Mozart No. 19 in F (K. 459), Solomon in Beethoven's G major, Myra Hess in Schumann and Denis Matthews in Beethoven's B flat. The guest conductors were Pedro Freitas Branco, who brought Turina and Falla besides Brahms's D minor Piano Concerto (Colin Horsley), Julius Harrison, Sargent (*Messiah* at Belle Vue with a famous quartet of soloists, Isobel Baillie, Gladys Ripley, Heddle Nash and Norman Walker) and Basil Cameron, who introduced to Manchester Vaughan Williams's Fifth Symphony, which had had its first performance only seven months earlier. It was an impressive range of music, and after the close of the Manchester series, Barbirolli took the orchestra to London in May 1944 to play to war workers, and at a Royal Philharmonic Society concert in the Royal Albert Hall on 26 May. An *Observer* writer said that already the new Hallé 'by general consent can take its place among the leading orchestras of the world'. A week later, on the anniversary of his arrival in Manchester, Barbirolli told the *Manchester Evening News*: 'I must be enabled to produce and maintain the finest orchestra (after the war I want an orchestra of at least ninety players) able to play to the widest public, if need be at uneconomic prices. A grant of some sort seems inevitable . . . Frankly, my stay in Manchester will depend on whether my ambitions for the orchestra are reciprocated – ambitions which are not personal to myself so much as to the interests of the city. One day I hope I shall see the city realise what a great and powerful advertising medium the Hallé has been, is and will continue to be for Manchester the world over. After the war I shall be extremely disappointed if such powers as might be responsible do not see to it that the orchestra is sent abroad . . . When we enlarge the orchestra after the war, first consideration will be given to men prevented from applying [in 1943] because of their service. But I cannot be expected to disturb the magnificent string ensemble laid down during the past year merely for sex reasons.'

As soon as Barbirolli had re-formed the orchestra, he turned his attention to finance and administration. Five days before his arrival, the Hallé committee had begun talks with Manchester Corporation representatives about possible civic aid to the orchestra. This led to a grant of £2,500, of which £1,000 was for children's concerts. Dakin of Sheffield, fearful lest his four-cities scheme should be forgotten, wrote directly to Barbirolli to interest him. Eventually Sheffield City Council

Associate conductors: George Weldon and Maurice Handford

Sir John Barbirolli: (*above*) on the opening night of his twenty-fifth season with Laurance Turner and Martin Milner (*left*) and Clive Smart (*right*); (*below*) entertaining sixteen Hallé gold medallists in 1963. *Left to right, front row*: Enid Roper, Norah Winstanley, Sir John, Lady Barbirolli, Pat Ryan; *second row*: Gladys Yates, Phyllis Greenhalgh, Sydney Partington, Tommy Cheetham, Alex Ferrier; *third row*: Oliver Bannister, Sydney Wright, Arthur Percival, Wally Jones, John Sullivan; *back*: Donald Shepherd, Arthur Shaw, Sydney Errington (both *Daily Telegraph*)

voted £5,000 to the Sheffield Philharmonic Society. It was not lost on the Hallé and Barbirolli that in 1944 Birmingham voted £14,000 to the city's symphony orchestra. Barbirolli, in a memorandum to the Hallé committee in January 1944, based on his experiences with the orchestra outside Manchester, said: 'Does Manchester deserve the Hallé? The Lord Mayor of Birmingham, the mayors of Hanley, Wolverhampton, Rotherham and Sheffield all come to Hallé concerts. Has the Lord Mayor ever been to a Hallé concert? Have the civic dignitaries of Manchester ever shown the slightest interest in the Hallé?'

On 31 January 1944, Barbirolli told Godlee, 'I have given you a first-class orchestra, despite a tenth-class management'. He was dissatisfied with Hesselgrave, but made it clear that it must be the committee's decision whether he was retained or dismissed. He also demanded to see the 1944-5 schedule by 1 April. On this schedule he would base his decision whether to remain as conductor. The Hallé offer, it should be remembered, was the means by which he returned to Britain; his original intention was not to stay in Manchester much more than a year. Yet already, though he did not perhaps fully realise it, his Hallé 'mission' was enslaving him. Hesselgrave was offered the post of accountant to the Society which he refused. He then resigned. In March T. E. Bean, a former member of the *Manchester Guardian* circulation staff and a knowledgeable music-lover, was appointed secretary and general manager. He produced the 1944-5 schedule, showing the estimated cost of the orchestra for the coming season as £47,000. The 1943-4 season had made a profit of £2,679 and the orchestra had given 194 concerts, most of them conducted by Barbirolli. This was too heavy a burden. Yet Manchester claimed it was empowered only to give money for concerts 'given in buildings in Manchester' and fifty concerts must be given in the city. Bean's first task, therefore, after successfully negotiating a new contract with the orchestra, was to find it a home in the city. Manchester districts were the only places in which the 'new' Hallé had so far never had to use a 'house full' board: this was attributed to the distances people had to travel to suburban cinemas. Bean arranged that the 1944-5 season should comprise twelve fortnightly Wednesday concerts in the Albert Hall, a Methodist church in Peter Street opposite the burned-out Free Trade Hall, and twelve Sunday afternoon concerts in the King's Hall, Belle Vue. The Albert Hall held only 1,750 people and on the day booking for the season opened a queue formed outside the Hallé's new offices at 8 St Peter's Square, at 5 a.m. Every ticket for the whole series was sold on the first day.

Within the space of a year Barbirolli had caught the imagination of the Manchester public and of concert-goers everywhere the Hallé played. In those days he was rather tubby and his hair was black. He was an exciting conductor to watch, his gestures expressive and beautiful. 'I see him now,' the composer Ronald Stevenson remembered,[1] 'his left hand throbbing in an imaginary vibrato.' He walked to the rostrum in short steps, his left arm crossed Napoleonically over his chest, and began the National Anthem facing the audience, turning round to face the orchestra for the last half of the tune. He would wait to begin the programme until absolute silence prevailed and the leader signalled to him that the last arrivals had settled in their seats. If this process took unduly long, he would turn and glare ferociously at the offenders. (But he was magnanimous. Once, before Schoenberg's *Verklärte Nacht*, a couple stood at the side of the hall, not wishing to risk further opprobrium by finding their seats. 'You'd better sit down,' he said. 'It's a long piece.') In the old Eastbrook Hall, Bradford, where the Hallé played from 1944 until 1952, he usually went at the interval to talk to the children who sat high behind the orchestra. Even if a performance had gone awry, he would convince everybody afterwards – including himself – that it was the greatest they had given. In the rehearsal-room next morning, he showed that he had not really been deceived. A few diehards in Manchester wondered what all the fuss was about and sighed for Sargent, but the players had no doubts. Whatever Barbirolli demanded from them, he demanded twice as much from himself. His special relationship with them was forged on the long and tedious wartime and post-war journeys. Because petrol was rationed, the Hallé travelled by train or sometimes in hired buses. Barbirolli shared his players' discomforts and refused preferential treatment. He stood in train corridors. He queued in cafés. He remembered birthdays and produced a cake. He walked from the centre of Manchester in the early hours of the morning to his flat in Rusholme because there were no taxis to meet the trains, and even then would not go to bed but would begin work on bowing scores while his wife typed Hallé correspondence. Those of us who were privileged to hear those early performances will never forget them – they marked us for life. There had been splendid performances in the past, but these were different. The sparkle, the sheen, the exhilaration, the rich tone, the wonderful ensemble, the sheer excitement and enthusiasm bowled us over. Let another listener describe the effect: 'With Barbirolli at the helm, music

[1]*The Listener*, 6 August 1970, p. 189.

was always ... a participation, a journeying together, a shared experience ... He had the marvellous ability of making what was happening in the concert-hall seem at that moment to be the most vital thing in the world ... There have been times after a Barbirolli performance – many of them – when one has walked out of the concert-hall seemingly on air. Standing waiting for buses in the cold night air and the long journeys home did not seem to matter ... It was good to be young and a Hallé concert-goer in those days ...'[1]

For Barbirolli himself, the biggest boon was his partnership with Godlee. The two men, one very tall, the other very short, liked each other from the start. At the Godlees' home in Didsbury, Barbirolli played in string quartets with Philip and his daughters (who later became members of the Hallé). Both men loved music passionately and had limitless ambitions for the Hallé. Godlee saw his function as chairman to ensure that Barbirolli got what he wanted for the orchestra. He would let the committee argue and wrangle, and then declare: 'Well, that's settled then. We'll agree to the motion.' And they did. He was a benevolent dictator. Their friendship was to undergo a baptism of fire in the first public controversy in which Barbirolli involved the Hallé committee.

[1]M. Martin: 'Voyage of Discovery' in *Sir John Barbirolli: 80th Anniversary* (The Barbirolli Society, 1979), pp. 26-8.

VIII—*Presidential suite*

Barbirolli's relationship with Beecham had always been ambivalent. When they worked together at Covent Garden in the 1930s, Barbirolli alternately admired and despised the older man. He, the complete professional, found the 'amateur' aspect of Beecham hard to swallow. Oil and water. Thus, in 1935, he wrote to Evelyn Rothwell, before their marriage: 'T. B. referred to the whole show last night [*Tristan* at Covent Garden conducted by Beecham] as "the most extraordinary series of sounds I have heard during the last fifteen years". But it is not quite so funny when you realise he can be amused by what was in reality a sacrilege and an agony for any decent musician. What a mixture he is.'

In January 1936 Beecham guest-conducted ten concerts by the New York Philharmonic. His engagement had infuriated the orchestra's musical director, Toscanini, whose opinion of him was summed up in the words 'clown and buffoon'. After Beecham's first appearances with this orchestra in 1932, Toscanini had expressly forbidden his re-engagement. It was the New York management's defiance of this veto that led to Toscanini's resignation before the 1936-7 season and, ironically, to Barbirolli's summons to New York.[1] Probably such a long spell as ten concerts encouraged Beecham to believe that the permanent post might be his. The next thing he knew, it was to be filled by the young man who had been his assistant. He wrote to Arthur Judson, administrator of the New York Philharmonic, and to several of its influential patrons, expressing surprise that such a post should be offered to a conductor with such little international experience. Some of the recipients had no more sense than to show these letters to Barbirolli, and Judson told him that Beecham's fury was unbelievable and that he had had letters one would hardly believe possible. To Barbirolli, the idea that a fellow-countryman could behave in such a way towards a colleague in a foreign country was unforgivable, and he never did forgive him. Early in 1943, in Barbirolli's last New York season, Beecham described the Philharmonic as 'almost as bad' as one of the London orchestras he had once had to revive. To the conductor of this orchestra for the previous seven years, this was the crowning insult.

What Barbirolli did not know when he became Hallé conductor was that the Society had a president – Sir Thomas Beecham, Bart. He had held the office since 1934, when Elgar had died. The post was honorary and involved no particular duties. Early in 1944, Beecham announced that he would be returning to England from America, where he had been since 1940, for a short tour. He informed the Hallé committee that he would be able to conduct one of their Manchester concerts. When Godlee reported this to Barbirolli, the response was: 'If you let that man near my orchestra, you won't see my arse for dust.' He then advised Godlee to find a new president, the sooner the better. He did not care *how* he did it, as long as he did it. Poor Godlee, in an impossible position, and unable to state the real reasons for the situation, thought up a ruse, though it was to prove inept. The committee decided on 5 July 1944 that, at the annual meeting in December, the chairman should move that the Lord Mayor of Manchester be invited to become president 'by virtue of his office'. Godlee then wrote to Beecham in New York on 17 July explaining the proposed change in the light of anxiety 'to strengthen the link with the Corporation' in pursuit of financial backing. The office of president, he somewhat ingenuously explained, had been allowed to lapse after 1940 'owing to the difficulty

[1]See Harvey Sachs, *Toscanini* (London, 1978), pp. 241-2.

of maintaining touch with you and our ignorance of your future movements'.

Beecham did not reply. On 25 October he told the Press that the Hallé had 'deposed' him. This was 'atrocious manners' and he took no further interest in the Society, which had had as much opportunity to communicate with him since 1940 as 'hundreds of other people in Great Britain'. His supporters rallied and in November a motion was received for the annual meeting proposing that the presidency had not lapsed and that Beecham's appointment 'originally affirmed at a previous general meeting' should continue. In fact, Bean discovered that the appointment was made at a committee meeting on 5 March 1934 but no reference to the presidency appeared in the minutes of the 1934 annual meeting, in the annual report or in any subsequent minutes or reports. Meanwhile Forbes, a friend of Beecham, met him and found him conciliatory and willing to meet Barbirolli. Forbes persuaded Barbirolli to write 'a cordial letter' to Beecham. This was a magnanimous gesture by Barbirolli to help Godlee; but when the letter was not even acknowledged he would give no further ground.

At the annual meeting on 12 December, the presidency issue was deferred until an extraordinary meeting so that a new approach to Beecham could be made. Beecham was to conduct in Liverpool on 15 December and agreed to meet Bean at the Adelphi Hotel after the concert. Bean described the encounter in a letter to Godlee written that night: 'It was a glorious and ignominious failure! Beecham is deriving far too much pleasure from kicking the Hallé committee all over the ground to relinquish the ball just yet. He preached, he fumed, he fulminated with such a simulation of passion, conviction and outraged virtue that there were moments when I really began to think that he actually meant and felt all he said . . . To establish a footing of complete frankness, and to put me at my ease, he began by expressing the opinion that the Hallé Concerts Society had the manners of a skunk, the spirit of a louse and the conscience of a badger! . . . "I will never conduct the Hallé Orchestra until Manchester has rid herself of that ridiculous body, the Hallé Committee" . . . As the tornado swept over my head, surpassing in velocity anything I have ever heard in the way of invective, I had the exhilarated feeling of one watching a gusty Restoration comedy not only being acted but improvised on the spot . . .' Only once, Bean reported, 'behind his cascades of invective and rhetorical largesse did I feel a genuine spring of belief'. This was when Beecham 'suddenly pointed an imperative digit at me (I almost broke into a bassoon solo in response to the familiar gesture!) and thundered out' a threat to serve each member of the committee with a writ and 'hold up the Society for five years in chancery'. Bean then summed up the position: 'It is obvious that Beecham does not want a solution. He needs some fight on his hands as an outlet for his abounding energy . . . He threatens to tell all the newspapers in America what he claims is the common property of everyone in this country . . . namely, that the Hallé Society has made itself ridiculous as well as dishonest by allowing its policy to be dictated by that upstart, Barbirolli. In the light of all the vituperation he spat at J. B. I am puzzled to explain his charm and reasonableness to Mr Forbes on the question of J. B. . . . If he jockeys us into making solemn statements and resting our case on thin subterfuges he'll make rings round us. On the question of the presidency, Tommy has won the first round – handsomely. We can't now embroil the Lord Mayor in this farcical comedy. But in view of the fact that we have an extraordinary meeting on our hands, some course of action *must* be decided upon.'

Five days later Bean left England with the Hallé and Barbirolli for a concert tour of the Western Front, where Allied troops had been fighting since the D-Day invasion on 6 June. The Beecham affair predominated as far as Barbirolli was concerned. On the train to Folkestone on 20 December, Bean wrote to Godlee: 'J. B. naturally wanted to know what had happened at Liverpool. The account – even in an expurgated form – caused something like an earthquake. I am afraid any hope of even a face-saving reconciliation is gone . . . J. B. is all for bringing the fight into the light of day, letting it be known what T. B. has said and so finishing the business . . .' Next day, Bean wrote again: 'His [Barbirolli's] solution is to report to the [extraordinary general] meeting as much as possible of what B. said about himself. He's tired of the intrigue and whispered insinuation, and is prepared to leave the public to judge the merits of the case . . . He is writing to America for the evidence of T. B.'s "sliminess".'

By the time the Hallé committee met on 31 January, Bean and Godlee had discovered that no legal basis existed for the office of president because there was no provision for it in the Society's articles of association, therefore they urged the committee to propose to the extraordinary meeting that the office should be left in abeyance until the Society's constitution, already under review, had been amended. Beecham's principal champion in Manchester, Caspar Quas-Cohen, was told of this legal development and agreed to submit a resolution in almost identical terms. He had previously warned the committee that if the election of the Lord Mayor was proposed, he would move for Beecham's continuation in office, would say that the real reason for the controversy was 'the personal vendetta of Barbirolli' and, if defeated,

46

would send to the Press a letter from Beecham attacking Barbirolli and the committee. The extraordinary meeting was fixed for 9 February. On 6 February the *Manchester Guardian* published a long letter from Beecham reviewing the history of his 'deposal' and stating that he regarded himself as president henceforward. If the Hallé meeting elected another president, he said, they would 'enjoy the uncommon advantage of two presidents instead of one . . . For one hundred years during the Middle Ages Christendom beheld the edifying spectacle of rival Popes, one in Rome and the other in Avignon . . . Yet so far as I can read, the cause of religion does not appear to have suffered from this division of authority . . .' The *Guardian* accompanied this with a leader which called the affair 'a comic strip' and 'an undignified personal squabble' and supported Beecham.

The comedy ended at the extraordinary meeting. Godlee, in a speech written for him by Bean, dealt lightly and wittily with the events of the previous six months. The Quas-Cohen resolution calling for new articles of association was carried unanimously. When the new constitution of the Society was published in December 1946, there was still no provision for a president and nobody challenged the matter. The office was quietly laid to rest.

Bean, Godlee and Beecham had probably enjoyed the exchange of polemics. They were playing games, because all knew that the root cause of the situation was unlikely to be made public. Just how serious Beecham was with his threat of legal action cannot be known. Bean recalled, in a letter to me, how he took his draft of the Hallé statement at the extraordinary meeting to Godlee, who scrutinised it 'through that ironically discerning monocle of his, through which he viewed the quirks and follies of mankind. He added, if I remember correctly, three commas and a semicolon. And then, with an anticipatory chuckle at the fun in store (for he always had a predilection for the calculated indiscretion over the more sober utterances of statesmanship) he adopted the statement *in toto* . . . and, without consulting the committee, duly presented it to that most extraordinary extraordinary meeting – his last act of benevolent despotism before the promised "democratisation" of the Society could take effect.'

Bean, pitched into this palaver within weeks of taking up his post, maintained a coolly detached view of the protagonists, but had no doubt that Barbirolli's attitude was understandable. He regarded the New York episode as 'quite indefensible' and formed the view, during his Liverpool interview with Beecham, that if he had thought Barbirolli's dislike of Beecham unduly strong, even when he knew the good reasons for it, it was 'nothing at all compared with T.B.'s stupid, almost pathological dislike' of Barbirolli. He felt, later, that his rôle in the affair 'must have seemed to John more than a little ambivalent, for while I was partly aware of the unscrupulously Macchiavellian lengths to which T. B. could go in denigrating his colleagues, I couldn't take his villainy all that seriously – off the podium! I knew what a rascal he could be in his professional relationships: but then I knew what a sublime artist he could be when he had only Mozart or Handel or Delius to deal with, and I tended to think that the latter was of more importance.'

Godlee and Bean had pulled the Hallé's chestnuts out of the fire, no mean feat considering the ineptitude of the original attempt to involve the Lord Mayor. But other members of the Hallé committee, principally Forbes and Leonard Behrens, who had not been consulted on tactics, still wanted – after the extraordinary meeting – to appease Beecham by inviting him to conduct the Hallé in Manchester. Bean was given the thankless task of trying to win Barbirolli's approval. At the same time, these committee members referred to the 'second-rate guest conductors being engaged', with the implication that Barbirolli resented or feared comparison with the best. Barbirolli was adamant. He had offered once to conciliate Beecham and had been snubbed. He would not offer again. He distrusted him and he refused to allow him near the Hallé. If the Hallé Society wanted him, let them invite him with another orchestra. As for the guest conductors, he had suggested the two best (reputedly) French conductors as these were the only European guests then available. When conditions returned to normal, he would be the first to welcome all distinguished conductors as guests, such as Bruno Walter, Erich Kleiber and others. He probably did not know that Walter had offered the committee a conducting date for 10 November 1945 at a fee of 200 guineas. The Hallé invited him for 100 guineas. He did not accept.

Beecham did not conduct in Manchester until 1948, when he conducted two public concerts by the B. B.C. Northern Orchestra in the Albert Hall. In December of the same year he took his own Royal Philharmonic Orchestra, which he had formed in 1946, to Belle Vue. In a hall which could accommodate six thousand, he was insulted by the number of two thousand who attended and said: 'I have not had a good audience in Manchester for thirty years [i.e. since 1918, which is hard to believe]. As far as I am concerned it is the worst city in England. Any third-rate foreigner can come here and get a good audience. Look what they do to me. I am nearly seventy, and I am tired of playing to savages.'[1] He was not invited under Hallé auspices until 1955, when he again conducted the R.P.O.

[1]*The Daily Telegraph*, 7 December 1948.

48

IX—*After the war*

The Beecham affair has taken us ahead of chronological sequence. Before the 1944-5 season in the Albert Hall began, Barbirolli was guest at a civic lunch in Manchester Town Hall. He pleaded for much greater civic aid to the orchestra and for the city to send the orchestra overseas after the war as 'ambassadors of trade as well as of art'. He told the councillors not to think of him as a modern Oliver Twist. 'Unlike Oliver, I would not ask for more. I would ask for a lot more.'

He was to take the Hallé overseas, for the first time in its history, before the war ended. In December 1944, the orchestra went to play to British troops in Holland and Belgium. The tour was arranged by Walter Legge, then director of music for E.N.S.A. Seventeen concerts were given in fifteen days: seven in Eindhoven, two in Lille, several in Brussels and one in Ostend. In the troopship crossing the Channel, many of the orchestra and Barbirolli himself slept on deck in bitter weather. Eindhoven was almost in the front line of the Ardennes offensive and after one concert the town was machine-gunned by German aircraft. Soldiers from the battlefront sat in their dirty battledress to listen to the music, calling for encore after encore. Solomon, the pianist, Arthur Grumiaux, the violinist, and Joan Hammond, the soprano, were soloists during the fortnight. Barbirolli described the visit many years later as 'perhaps the happiest and most inspiring fortnight the orchestra and I have ever spent together'.

During the 1944-5 season the Hallé gave 258 concerts, a punishing schedule. The Albert Hall series in Manchester included the seven symphonies of Sibelius. There was a strong representation of French music, with Ravel's *Shéhérazade* (Olive Groves, soprano), the Piano Concerto for left hand (Clifford Curzon) and *Daphnis and Chloë*. Richard Strauss's *Don Quixote, Tod und Verklärung*, and *Le bourgeois gentilhomme* were played. R. J. Forbes was soloist in Delius's Piano Concerto and Sammons in the Violin Concerto. In Brahms's Double Concerto the soloists were two Hallé principals, Laurance Turner and Haydn Rogerson. At Belle Vue, Barbirolli conducted Elgar's Second Symphony (having first conducted his 'new' Hallé in this work at Sheffield on 12 January 1945) and Verdi's *Requiem*, a performance dedicated to the memory of Franklin D. Roosevelt, who had just died in office as American President. Guest conductors were Sargent and Albert Coates, who conducted the first Hallé performance of

Shostakovich's Fifth Symphony on 28 February 1945. When Barbirolli conducted *Le bourgeois gentilhomme* at Sheffield, he thought the applause was cool, so he explained the history of the work to the audience, described features of its brilliant scoring, and played it again. Before the Manchester season began he lectured on the programmes, and Manchester University arranged twelve lecture-recitals during the season.

At the committee meeting on 21 March 1945, Bean reported what was to be a *leitmotiv* of Barbirolli's conductorship: deep concern that, under existing rates of pay, he was finding it difficult to attract and retain the best available players. A new contract was therefore negotiated with basic salaries of £15 a week for principals, £12 for sub-principals and £10 for rank-and-file. In December 1945, at the annual meeting, Godlee presented the long-promised 'democratisation' of the Society. The £10 guarantee was abolished. There was to be a new class of full membership, lasting ten years, on payment of £9 or five yearly payments of £2. Membership at this time was down to eighty-four. The *Manchester Evening News* hailed the new scheme as a means of presenting a stronger case to the city council. The engagement of Barbirolli, the writer said, was the first outward sign of the revival of Manchester from its decline in the 1930s. 'A great new Manchester without the Hallé Orchestra is impossible to imagine.' This was the immediate post-war mood epitomised by Barbirolli's word-picture of 'a great orchestra and a great public walking hand in hand, treading paths familiar and unfamiliar, and discovering together in close companionship pleasure and at times exaltation'. Another symbol of the revived interest in the Hallé was the formation of the Hallé Club (in football parlance a supporters' club). Priority booking, though later withdrawn, was a prime attraction to join, but the various branches organised lectures and other activities to stimulate interest in the orchestra. In August 1946 publication of the Society's magazine *Hallé* began. Ernest Bean, John Boulton and Arnold Dowbiggin were the editorial board and articles came from distinguished contributors, among them Cardus, still in Australia where reports of the Hallé revival had reached him. 'What is Manchester doing to deserve this great Hallé Orchestra?' he asked.

A pertinent question. In September 1946 Godlee and Bean went to the Town Hall to present the Hallé's case for a guarantee against an expected loss of £3,700 on the 1946-7 season. Godlee rested his case on the Society's chief asset, its conductor. He said to the municipal representatives: 'Not a week passes without an invitation to him to conduct other orchestras in other towns at fees ranging from 150 to 300 guineas a concert. Yet because he prefers solid achievement to flashy appearances, he has turned them down and been happy to conduct the Hallé, under far from ideal conditions, at a fee which averages less than 25 guineas a concert – the lowest rate paid by any orchestra in this country. During the past few weeks . . . the leading London orchestra [London Symphony] has offered him the post of music director with a completely free hand in the direction of policy, with a promise to establish an orchestra of ninety players (as compared with the Hallé strength of seventy) and with a salary of over £6,000 a year. Barbirolli (though, like the rest of us, he is not anxious to under-sell his services) is ready to stay in Manchester for a salary less than he can secure elsewhere provided that we give him the chance that he wants – the chance of making the Hallé the greatest orchestra in the country and comparable with the best in the world . . . In the opinion of the Hallé committee, he is the linchpin of the orchestra's success.' Godlee asked the council for a guarantee of up to £15,000 a year and suggested that the corporation should present the situation to the public so that ratepayers could see that the city had taken a lead. A month later Barbirolli attended a Hallé committee meeting and urged a further increase in the players' salaries (£20, £15 and £12). He also pleaded for an annual overseas tour.

In rejecting the L.S.O. offer, Barbirolli said that 'my duty lies with the orchestra it has been my privilege to recreate. I should like to feel we are on the verge of great things.' When his decision was made public, he was given a tremendous ovation at a Belle Vue concert. He said to his wife: 'I simply can't leave that'. The 1945-6 Albert Hall series had been widened to comprise fifteen Tuesday concerts, with the programme duplicated on Wednesday, and twenty-two at Belle Vue. Even with double the number of seats available at the Albert Hall, every season ticket was again sold on the first day of booking. Thus, for the first time in its history, the orchestra gave fifty-two concerts in Manchester in a season. Yet its total number of concerts in 1945-6 was 224 (at a profit of £444), an indication of how it had become a truly national orchestra. Beethoven was the foundation of the Belle Vue concerts – the nine symphonies, five piano concertos, violin concerto, and four overtures. At the Albert Hall the four Brahms symphonies were played and Barbirolli conducted Elgar's *Falstaff*, the first performance in England of Martinu's First Symphony (16 October), Falla's *Nights in the Gardens of Spain*, with Curzon as solo·pianist, Debussy's *La Mer*, Strauss's *Don Quixote*, Gordon Jacob's Clarinet Concerto, Bach's Double Violin Concerto, Bax's *The Garden of Fand*, extracts from Act I and the complete Act II of Wagner's *Tristan und*

Isolde, with Edna Hobson as Isolde, Walter Widdop as Tristan, Janet Howe as Brangäne and Norman Walker as King Mark, Ireland's Piano Concerto (Kendall Taylor), Moeran's Violin Concerto (Albert Sammons), Strauss's *Till Eulenspiegel*, Stravinsky's *Petrushka*, Vaughan Williams's *Tallis Fantasia* and, on 9 and 10 April, Mahler's *Das Lied von der Erde*, with Catherine Lawson and Parry Jones as the soloists. On 23 April four of the orchestral violinists were soloists in Vivaldi's concerto for four violins and Barbirolli introduced Delius's *North Country Sketches* to the concerts. In his Belle Vue programmes Barbirolli conducted Elgar's First Symphony, Lalo's *Symphonie espagnole* with Jacques Thibaud as soloist (Thibaud had also played Mozart and Saint-Saëns at the Albert Hall), Haydn's D major and Dvořák's Cello Concertos, with Casals as soloist (28 October), Acts I and II of *Aida*, with the *Tristan* soloists and Dennis Noble as Amonasro, Verdi's *Requiem* (Joan Hammond, Gladys Ripley, Parry Jones and Tom Williams), and a Viennese concert in which Mozart arias and duets were sung by Norah Gruhn and Percy Heming. Guest conductors included Reginald Goodall, who introduced Britten's *Sea Interludes* from *Peter Grimes* to Manchester (26 March) and also conducted Sibelius's *Tapiola* and Schumann's Second Symphony, Sargent (*Messiah* and a visit with the Liverpool Philharmonic which included Elgar's Second Symphony and the first Manchester performance of Bartók's Second Violin Concerto, with Max Rostal as soloist), George Weldon (Walton's First Symphony), Constant Lambert (Vaughan Williams's Fifth Symphony and his own *Aubade héroique* and *Horoscope* suite), Heinz Unger, who risked only the first movement of Bruckner's Fourth Symphony forty-one years after Richter had done it all, Anthony Collins and Enrique Jorda. Among the soloists not already mentioned were Ida Haendel, Ginette Neveu (Brahms concerto with Goodall), Maurice Raskin and Arthur Grumiaux (violinists) and the pianists Moiseiwitsch, Solomon, Cyril Smith, Louis Kentner, R. J. Forbes, and Shulamith Shafir. In *Messiah* the soloists were Isobel Baillie, Peter Pears, Norman Walker, and, making her first Hallé appearance in Manchester (9 December 1945), Kathleen Ferrier. Later in this season, in the Sheffield series, on 26 April 1946, Barbirolli conducted Elgar's *The Dream of Gerontius* for the first time, with Ferrier, Parry Jones and David Franklin. He had not been impressed by Ferrier a year earlier when, also at Sheffield, she sang Elgar's *Sea Pictures*. But in *Gerontius* he wholeheartedly admired her and there began a close personal friendship with the woman he called 'my beloved Katie'.

The financial approaches to Manchester Corporation were made against the background of important developments in Yorkshire, where Leeds and other towns had joined to support a new Symphony Orchestra. Sheffield, even though it had no say in running Hallé affairs, declined to join the Yorkshire scheme and stayed loyal to the Hallé. (In the 1947-8 Sheffield season of Hallé concerts, over a hundred thousand people attended and at twenty of the concerts people were turned away.) The new Y.S.O. received civic aid of £35,000 a year, and its top price for some concerts was only half-a-crown. Manchester's response in July 1947 was to offer the Hallé Society £6,000 for fourteen children's concerts and £9,000 guarantee against loss for the 1947-8 season. In return, three councillors were to have seats on the Hallé committee. The Hallé agreed; there were hopes, too, of an extra £5,000 guarantee from the Arts Council (successor to the wartime C.E.M.A.). Deficit on the 1946-7 season had been £985, and the total of 242 concerts was still regarded as too high for the good of the orchestra's playing standards. Not that these seemed to be unduly endangered by so much work. The orchestra was much in demand for the festivals which were springing up in a Britain still living in austere post-war economic conditions. When it played at the first Edinburgh Festival in 1947, Cardus, who had recently returned from Australia, wrote in the *Manchester Guardian*: 'Here is a real orchestra, wanting only a small addition of players to elevate it to European class ... No part of Barbirolli's Hallé is greater than the whole: as Szigeti murmured last night as he listened: "They are all, every one of them, playing".' At the same festival a year later Ernest Newman stated that the Hallé compensated for poor performances by the Concertgebouw Orchestra of Amsterdam. Barbirolli, he wrote, 'has developed into a conductor of international front rank'. At the 1947 Leeds Festival, Barbirolli conducted Beethoven's Ninth Symphony and Verdi's *Requiem*, with the soprano parts sung by Ljuba Welitsch. In 1947, too, the Hallé began its long association with the Cheltenham Festival of British Contemporary Music, giving over the next eleven years many first performances of British symphonies and concertos. Yet H.M.V. recordings of this orchestra and its conductor were still issued only on the cheap plum label; not until 1949 was it regarded as worthy of the international red-label series.

For the Hallé's first peace-time overseas visit, plans were made for it to play at the Prague Festival in 1948. The Communist takeover in Czechoslovakia meant rapid reorganisation and an Austrian tour was arranged instead for May–June 1948. Concerts were given in Innsbruck, Salzburg (in the Mozarteum, where Evelyn Rothwell gave the first performance of the recently discovered Mozart Oboe Concerto, hitherto known only in its transposition from C to D as the

Flute Concerto, K. 314), Graz and Vienna. Elgar's *Enigma Variations* were played at each concert and the Viennese critics highly praised the two concerts given in the capital. On return to England, Barbirolli wrote to Godlee: 'It was a triumph won note by note . . . They are playing magnificently, with just that right amount of consciousness of their achievement to produce a real sense of mastery . . . We must face the fact that we now have an orchestra of a quality that you could not hope to get in the South at the terms we are able to pay . . . Offer a good but completely inexperienced player £15 a week to come to Manchester and they look at you as if you were barmy.' He was desperately anxious for Godlee to support him in his ambition for an annual overseas visit because he knew such opportunities helped to retain good players. Not only was there a drain of talent to the B.B.C. Symphony, London Symphony, Covent Garden and London Philharmonic Orchestras, but since 1945 and 1946 Walter Legge's Philharmonia and Beecham's Royal Philharmonic represented temptations.

In February 1948 the shrewd Bean wrote a memorandum to the committee about the renewal of Barbirolli's contract. If his services were to be retained, he said, a reduction below the 150 or more Hallé concerts a season he was conducting would have to be made in the interests both of his health and of giving him time to study new works. As for his salary, 'the average fee of £33 per concert is known to be lower than he could have obtained from other orchestras . . . This sacrifice of pecuniary advantage is not one which the Society would be wise to regard as a permanent basis of his engagement.' Bean suggested that in future Barbirolli should conduct 120 concerts a season, but as the orchestra's schedule was to be reduced from 240 to 192 concerts, this would not mean any increase in guest conductors' fees. Barbirolli, he said, would accept this instead of any salary increase. But, Bean said, there were factors which he had *not* discussed with Barbirolli. 'The salary of £5,000 per annum still represents only £41 per concert . . . From information in my possession, it seems highly probable that the B.B.C. will sooner or later seek to secure Mr Barbirolli as conductor of the B.B.C. Symphony Orchestra.' So should they not anticipate the offer and raise his salary now?

Bean's grapevine was well informed. In June, during the Cheltenham Festival, Steuart Wilson, B.B.C. Director of Music, offered the B.B.C. post to Barbirolli. Negotiations continued for the next few months, but the public were not told until the late autumn. There was intensive press interest, and in Manchester especially 'Will he go or will he stay?' was the question of the hour. It was known that the deadline for Barbirolli's decision was 31 December 1948. Godlee saw the chance for some valuable Hallé publicity and probably guessed, if he did not actually already know, what Barbirolli's decision would be. There is no doubt that Barbirolli felt greatly honoured by the invitation to succeed Boult and realised he would have a bigger orchestra and a lighter schedule. But he knew he was not by nature a 'studio' conductor and he must also have known that, whatever battles he had with the Hallé committee, these were preferable to B.B.C. bureaucracy. None the less, he was also aware of his value to the Hallé, and his decision to refuse the B.B.C. offer was probably made on 7 December when the Hallé committee promised him to increase the orchestra to ninety-six players when the Free Trade Hall was rebuilt, to increase rank-and-file pay to parity with the B.B.C. Northern Orchestra (£13 a week), to compete on equal terms with other orchestras in rates for principals, and to go abroad once a year. Barbirolli replied that he sought nothing for himself, only that the Hallé should become an 'international orchestra and not merely a provincial band'. If that ambition was accepted, he would stay for as long as he was wanted. His refusal to leave the Hallé caught the public imagination far outside Manchester, for there were editorials saluting his decision in the newspapers of several foreign countries.

The pro-Hallé fervour generated by Barbirolli's decision took membership of the Society to over 1,200 by the 1949-50 season, aided by the energy and enthusiasm of the committee's honorary membership secretary, J H Thom. The 1948-9 season had resulted in a loss of £7,127, claimed from the corporation, and Alderman Abraham Moss, one of the city's representatives on the committee and a distinguished chairman of the education committee, proposed a conference of local authorities in Lancashire and Cheshire with a view to establishing the Hallé and Liverpool Philharmonic on a sound financial basis. Various towns visited by the Hallé offered guarantees against loss on these concerts. The Arts Council increased its grant to £10,000. Things were looking up. The Hallé committee's reference, in their promises to Barbirolli, to a rebuilt Free Trade Hall was the result of a decision taken by the Town Hall Committee in July 1948. Five months later, Whitehall refused the application because there was still a strict limit on steel allocation, but in February 1949 the decision was reversed. In April 1949, the Hallé went to Holland in an exchange visit with The Hague Residentie Orchestra. Three concerts were given in The Hague and one in Leiden. In The Hague the soloist in Beethoven's Violin Concerto was Ginette Neveu. Then, in August, the Hallé gave two concerts in the Casino Communal, Knokke-le-Zoute, as part of

Belgium's Summer Festival. Vaughan Williams's newest symphony, his Sixth, was played – Barbirolli had made a speciality of this work. There was one significant difference between The Hague and Knokke visits: in Holland, the orchestra was conducted by Mr Barbirolli. In Belgium it was conducted by Sir John Barbirolli, as he had become in the June 1949 Birthday Honours.

Any tendency towards euphoria was to be swiftly dispelled on 30 December 1949, exactly a year after Barbirolli's rejection of the B.B.C., when the Corporation finance committee recommended a reduction in the Hallé guarantee-against-loss from £9,000 to £5,000 a year after July 1950 because of general 'financial stringency and restrictive measures'. Bean had estimated that the cost of fulfilling the pledges to Barbirolli would be as much as £19,000 extra a year, so the city's threat was a major blow. The anti-Hallé faction was led by Councillor J. E. Pheasey, who said that the orchestra was 'nothing like so popular as it is cracked up to be . . . I have read that Sir John Barbirolli may leave. I would say to Sir John that Manchester City Council has no responsibilities in this matter and the sooner you get your skates on and travel, the sooner you will be satisfied.' Another said that 'people like Barbirolli and Beecham have come back from America with big ideas, but we are not a rich and prosperous country'. Nationwide press comment chided Manchester for its attitude and Bolton decided to make the orchestra an outright grant. Preston followed this lead. Barbirolli pointed out that Manchester enjoyed a first-class orchestra at a cost far below that of any comparable orchestra in the world. 'If Manchester wants a little orchestra run by men with little ideas I agree that I and my colleagues are not the men for the job.' Pheasey, at a council debate on 24 May 1950, tried to have the already promised £9,000 guarantee for 1949-50 reduced to £5,000 'for this year only'. He was defeated – and a good thing, too, for the deficit on the 1949-50 season was £9,436.

Finance was only one of the continuing anxieties of 1950. Another was Barbirolli's health. In February 1949 he had to rest because of 'nervous gastritis'. Later that year his doctor persuaded him – and it can have been no easy task – to cancel all but Hallé engagements for a year (of course, after five months he was accepting guest engagements again!). The strain of over 250 concerts a year since 1943 and his régime of one meal a day, little sleep, heavy smoking and constant study of scores had begun to exact a toll. In addition, there was his growing disquiet over the administration of the Hallé by Bean, whom he felt to be too 'Civil Service' in his methods ('everything in 50-tuplicate', he used to say). It can now be said that Barbirolli's disenchantment with Bean was fostered by the man who since 1947

Sir John Barbirolli: (*above*) with (*left to right*) Lady Barbirolli, Philip Godlee and the violinist Ginette Neveu a few days before her tragic death; (*below*) with Sir Neville Cardus after a Manchester concert on 14 April 1966 in honour of Cardus's fifty years with the *Guardian*

Barbirolli conducting: (*above*) in 1948 at the Albert Hall, Manchester; (*below*) in about 1953

had been his personal manager, Kenneth E. Crickmore. This Mancunian ex-airman, after being invalided from the R.A.F. in 1943, had at twenty-three become administrator of Sheffield Philharmonic Society in 1944. Barbirolli was impressed by his wide knowledge of the orchestral repertoire, his gift for programme-planning and his attitude to the financing of music. He was devoted to this young man and blindly loyal to him. Many people, however, found Crickmore himself and his methods distinctly 'off side', and he made Barbirolli more enemies than friends because people did not trust him. If Crickmore wanted to go from A to B, it would always be via X, Y and Z. Individuals were treated as pawns in whatever conspiratorial game was afoot.

Writing to Godlee from Italy in 1950, Barbirolli indulged in 'a little plain speaking' to his friend, having previously written to Bean about his dissatisfaction with the administrative machinery. 'There is no suggestion', he wrote to Godlee, 'of any kind of a veiled request for his removal or resignation; rather do I feel as if someone for whose gifts I had the highest admiration, and for whom I have a great personal affection, is squandering his energies because of some blind spot . . . I have no wish to enter the Halle's administrative affairs. The colossal and continuous physical strain of rehearsals and performance, week after week and month after month, are about as much as I can stand, and unless I can feel more secure and serene as to what goes on behind me, I should have no alternative but to give up, as you can see from my present state of health . . . Sometimes I feel decisions are taken without consulting me which it takes me much time and tact to undo . . . The devotion of everyone to the "cause" must not be put in jeopardy for lack of a little plain speaking now.'

He urged a thorough reorganisation, with a concerts manager and a publicity officer. (Characteristically he added: 'So far there has not been much need of the latter as the orchestra's success and my notoriety!! have publicised themselves.') His fear was that Bean would not delegate responsibility to them, and he asked Godlee to make sure that he (Barbirolli) was kept fully informed of all recommendations to the committee from Bean. Godlee formed a sub-committee to give effect to Barbirolli's decisions and replied: 'Our one desire is to supply you with the organisation behind you which you asked for (and I promised you) in 1944. It is a matter of great grief to me that our efforts at the moment have worn thin or even broken down . . . I am personally in a hole. You have lost confidence in T.E.B. (as far as detailed administration goes) and the committee thinks he is indispensable. I have to produce a working arrangement between the two extremes.' The committee's pro-Bean faction was headed by Leonard Behrens, the treasurer, to whom both Godlee and Barbirolli were inimical.

Pleasanter aspects of 1950 were the awards to Barbirolli of an honorary doctorate of music by Manchester University and of the Gold Medal of the Royal Philharmonic Society, presented to him at a Hallé concert in London on 13 December by Vaughan Williams, who described him as 'one of those wizards who can take the dry bones of crotchets and quavers and breathe into them the breath of life'. In November of that year, the orchestra gave nine concerts in a thirteen-day tour of Portugal, playing in Lisbon, Aveira, Braga and Oporto. Besides Sibelius's Second and Vaughan Williams's Sixth Symphonies, works by Elgar, Delius, Roussel, Ravel, Debussy, Turina and Haydn were performed.

The year 1951 was chosen for the Festival of Britain, in which the country was to 'blow its own trumpet' in artistic and other matters and for which London was to gain a new concert-hall on the South Bank, the Royal Festival Hall. Various festival centres outside London were chosen, Liverpool being preferred to Manchester. But Manchester planned its own contribution by re-opening the Free Trade Hall towards the end of the year. A heavy schedule lay ahead for the Hallé, but in March, on his return from Australian engagements, Barbirolli had an appendicitis operation followed by a seven-week convalescence. In July Bean resigned from the Hallé to become manager of the Festival Hall. Barbirolli wanted Crickmore as the next Hallé manager (although Crickmore was not anxious to leave Sheffield). Behrens and his followers opposed the move and decided that the post should be put out to tender. This decision was taken at an August committee meeting while Godlee was on holiday and neither he nor Barbirolli had been consulted. Barbirolli's reaction, in a letter to Godlee almost certainly inspired, if not written, by Crickmore, was to say: 'We can discuss the pros and cons of putting it to tender when we meet tomorrow, but I do want you to bear the following in mind very seriously. Through Bean's dilatoriness in presenting it, I have not yet signed my contract, and I do assure you and the committee that I have no intention of doing so until I know what your decision is likely to be in the matter of choosing the man with whom I shall have to work in close co-operation for many years to come, *I hope'*. Crickmore was appointed. Seeing the division in the committee, he resigned but was then reappointed. Behrens resigned the treasurership and was succeeded by Sir James Lythgoe, former City Treasurer of Manchester. (In later years Barbirolli realised that he had allowed Crickmore to influence him unjustly against Bean and the breach was healed.)

The rebuilt Free Trade Hall was opened by the Queen (now Queen Elizabeth the Queen Mother) on Friday 16 November 1951. Its interior, with wooden panels and with sound-reflectors over the orchestra, is very much of its period, and the hall's drawbacks are all too apparent today, but in 1951 it seemed to be the attainment of a dream. At the short opening concert, Barbirolli conducted music by Maurice Johnstone and Vaughan Williams, Harty's arrangement of Handel's *Water Music* and his own *Elizabethan Suite*. Finally Kathleen Ferrier sang 'Land of Hope and Glory'. As Norman Shrapnel wrote in the *Manchester Guardian*, 'it was fine and it was right, but lovers of the tune will fear that never again can they hope to hear it in such glory. There were few dry eyes, as notices of such events used to say.' Next night Barbirolli conducted the *Meistersinger* overture, Walton's Viola Concerto (soloist, William Primrose) and Berlioz's *Symphonie fantastique*. Neville Cardus, revisiting a Manchester Hallé concert after more than a decade in Australia and London, was deeply moved by this 'night of resurrection in the desired paradise'. Seven more concerts followed in this inaugural festival. Two concerts were given by the Hamburg Radio Symphony Orchestra, conducted by Hans Schmidt-Isserstedt. Their programmes included Beethoven, Boccherini, Brahms, Liszt's A major Piano Concerto (soloist, Malcuzynski), Tippett's Double Concerto and Strauss's *Ein Heldenleben*. Eduard van Beinum conducted the Concertgebouw Orchestra of Amsterdam in two concerts, playing Bartók's *Concerto for Orchestra*, Wagner's *Five Wesendonck Songs* (Kirsten Flagstad the soloist), Haydn's 'Clock' Symphony and the first Manchester performance on 21 November of Bruckner's Eighth Symphony. Sargent conducted the B.B.C. Symphony Orchestra in Holst's *The Planets*, and the last two concerts were given by the Hallé. Barbirolli ended the celebration with Beethoven's Ninth Symphony, the four solo singers being Isobel Baillie, Marjorie Thomas, Richard Lewis and Norman Walker. It had been a week of music-making such as Manchester has rarely experienced. Before the Hallé's first Free Trade Hall season is reviewed, however, it is time to look back over the music-making of the previous five seasons in the Albert Hall and at Belle Vue.

The 1946-7 Albert Hall series was given on Wednesdays and Thursdays and the orchestra was increased to eighty players. Elgar's Second Symphony, Moeran's Cello Concerto with Peers Coetmore as soloist, Berlioz's *Harold in Italy*, Bax's Violin Concerto (Frederick Grinke), Rawsthorne's *Cortèges*, Debussy's *Ibéria*, Walton's Violin

Concerto (Thomas Matthews), the two *Daphnis* suites of Ravel, the Adagietto from Mahler's Fifth Symphony, Bruckner's Seventh Symphony, and Pitfield's *Sinfonietta* were among the works Barbirolli conducted, while at Belle Vue he conducted his first Manchester *Gerontius* on 30 March 1947 (with Gladys Ripley, Parry Jones and David Franklin), Schumann's Piano Concerto with Yvonne Arnaud, MacDowell's *Sonata Tragica* (an orchestration of this piano work by William Foote), and the Beethoven programme with which he customarily began this series. Sargent's concert with the Liverpool Philharmonic included Vaughan Williams's Oboe Concerto (Léon Goossens) and Britten's *Young Person's Guide to the Orchestra*, both new to the Hallé audience, and Rachmaninov's Third Symphony. Other guest conductors included Nicolai Malko, who revived Shostakovich's First Symphony, Enrique Jorda (the first Hallé performance since 1930 of Berlioz's *La Damnation de Faust*), and that engaging American anglophile Bernard Herrmann, who conducted Vaughan Williams's *A London Symphony*, Copland's *Billy the Kid* and his own suite *The Devil and Daniel Webster*. Memories of Harty's day were revived when Archie Camden returned to be soloist in Mozart's Bassoon Concerto under Barbirolli. Several of the 1947 Hallé's principals appeared as soloists during the season – Laurance Turner in Mendelssohn's Violin Concerto, Oliver Bannister in Bach's Suite in B minor for flute and strings, Elisabeth Hawkins in Handel's Oboe Concerto in B flat, George Alexander the solo viola part in *Harold in Italy*, and Pat Ryan in Mozart's Clarinet Concerto. Other soloists included Ginette Neveu, Alan Loveday and Raymond Cohen (violinists), Solomon, Curzon, Denis Matthews, Iso Elinson and Jan Smeterlin (pianists).

At the opening concert in the Albert Hall of the 1947-8 season Rudolf Serkin was soloist in Beethoven's C minor Piano Concerto and Barbirolli conducted Delius's *Dance Rhapsody* No. 1 and Sibelius's Fifth Symphony. At the second, Isobel Baillie gave the first Hallé performance of Finzi's *Dies Natalis*, with Barbirolli. Other Barbirolli specialities this season were Rawsthorne's *Street Corner* overture, Roussel's *Bacchus and Ariadne* Suite No. 2, Elgar's Violin Concerto (Thomas Matthews), Vaughan Williams's Fifth Symphony, Strauss's Oboe Concerto (Léon Goossens), extracts from *L'Enfance du Christ*, with Richard Lewis as solo tenor, as part of a Berlioz programme which included two scenes from *Romeo and Juliet* and *Harold in Italy*, Martinu's Cello Concerto, with Pierre Fournier, Sibelius's Violin Concerto (Henry Holst), Bartók's Third Piano Concerto (Kendall Taylor) and Britten's Violin Concerto (Theo Olof). For his Belle Vue Beethoven concert Barbirolli engaged Wolfgang Schneiderhan as soloist in the Violin

Concerto. Solomon was his soloist in Brahms's First Piano Concerto, Curzon in the Second (at the Albert Hall). Elgar's Second Symphony was given at Belle Vue, as was Philip Sainton's *The Island*. Neveu played the Brahms concerto at Belle Vue, with Barbirolli, a performance he compared with Kreisler's. In *Gerontius* on 21 March, Ferrier sang the Angel. The Hallé chorusmaster Herbert Bardgett revived Mendelssohn's *Elijah* at Belle Vue. Sargent, now Sir Malcolm, again brought the Liverpool Philharmonic (Holst's *The Planets*), and the other guest conductors were Josef Krips, who had Edwin Fischer as soloist in Mozart's C minor Piano Concerto (K. 491) and conducted Bruckner's Fourth Symphony complete, and Karl Rankl, then musical director of Covent Garden, who gave the first Hallé performance since 1927 of Mahler's Fourth Symphony, with Desi Halban as the soprano. At Rankl's Belle Vue concert the soloist in Tchaikovsky's First Piano Concerto was Gina Bachauer. Another Belle Vue event, on 25 April 1948, was Barbirolli's conducting of Act 3 (much cut) of Wagner's *The Mastersingers*, with Doris Doree as Eva, William Herbert as Walther and Tom Williams as Sachs. In the first half Herbert was soloist in Ireland's *These Things Shall Be*.

Brahms's symphonies were again all performed in the 1948-9 season, three in the Albert Hall series and No. 1 at Belle Vue. (Nos. 2 and 3 were conducted by Barbirolli, Nos. 1 and 4 by Fernando Previtali.) Barbirolli also conducted the Second Piano Concerto (Curzon) and the Double Concerto (Antonio Brosa and André Navarra). He opened the season in the Albert Hall with two first Hallé performances – Mahler's *Kindertotenlieder*, unforgettably sung by Ferrier, and Villa-Lobos's *Discovery of Brazil*. In October 1948 it was more of a novelty than it is today when the concerto was for guitar – Castelnuovo-Tedesco's, played by Segovia. Barbirolli preceded it with the first Hallé performance of Rossini's *Cenerentola* overture! And he conducted Debussy's *Printemps* in its first Manchester performance since 1914. The 'new' Mozart Oboe Concerto was played by Evelyn Rothwell on 24 and 25 November and Barbirolli revived Delius's *Eventyr*. Michael Krein was soloist in Phyllis Tate's Saxophone Concerto, which Barbirolli conducted. His programme for 12 and 13 January 1949 contained three works not previously performed by the Hallé – Schoenberg's *Verklärte Nacht*, Hindemith's symphony *Mathis der Maler* and Debussy's *Danse sacrée et danse profane*. The symphony, Schumann's Fourth, had not been played since 1936. He conducted Arthur Benjamin's Symphony on 26 and 27 January, the first Manchester performances of Rachmaninov's Fourth Piano Concerto (Iso Elinson) on 23 and 24 February and of Vaughan Williams's Sixth

Symphony on 9 and 10 March, and the first British performances, on 4 and 5 May, of Strauss's Duett Concertino for clarinet and bassoon (Pat Ryan and Charles Cracknell). At Belle Vue Barbirolli returned to Walton's *Façade* Suite No. 1 and conducted the 1946 version of Stravinsky's *Petrushka* (though he kept the original ending). Krips conducted Bruckner's Sixth Symphony on 10 and 11 November. Dinu Lipatti had been booked as soloist in Mozart's C major Piano Concerto (K. 467) for this concert, but his place was taken by Albert Ferber. (Lipatti died of leukaemia in 1950.) Rafael Kubelik brought back Dvořák's Seventh Symphony and Hugo Rignold's concert with the Liverpool Philharmonic included Elgar's *Falstaff*, Jean Françaix's Piano Concerto played by the composer, Walton's *Scapino* and Sibelius's *Tapiola*. The Belle Vue concert on 9 January now has an historic look – Lambert conducted his own *Rio Grande* and his friend Walton's *Belshazzar's Feast*, with the original baritone soloist Dennis Noble. This was only its second Hallé performance. The Boyd Neel String Orchestra played four (Nos. 2, 3, 4 and 5) of the Brandenburg Concertos of Bach. Nicolai Malko revived Borodin's Second Symphony and introduced Prokofiev's *Lieutenant Kije* suite, but it was Barbirolli who conducted Rachmaninov's Second Symphony, observing the cuts as he had in New York. Bardgett conducted Bach's Mass in B minor; and two concerts were given by The Hague Residentie Orchestra, conducted by Jan Out, who introduced the Third Symphony by Léon Orthel and also the Third Symphony by Schubert, apparently never before heard by a Hallé audience! Inevitably in these surveys only a few works can be mentioned, but one does not overlook the staple repertory of Tchaikovsky, Beethoven and Elgar. Barbirolli's favourite Beethoven symphonies were the Third, Fourth and (especially) the Seventh, but at this period he also conducted the 'Pastoral' more than he did later. Five Rossini overtures, not all conducted by him, were a feature of the 1948-9 season, and he conducted the first Hallé performance of Gounod's *Petite Symphonie* for wind instruments.

For the 1949-50 Albert Hall season Barbirolli, now Sir John, again conducted the Sibelius Symphonies in chronological order. These remain in the memory after nearly thirty-five years as vivid and revelatory performances, especially the magnificent programme which comprised Nos. 3, 4 and 5, like listening to the composer's autobiography in sound. At the first concerts in Manchester, Sheffield and Bradford, Ginette Neveu played Sibelius's Violin Concerto, a performance which for fiery intensity and poetic insight has still not been exceeded, if even equalled, in my experience. A few days later she was killed in an air crash. Barbirolli and the orchestra were stunned, for she had become a loved as well as admired colleague. On 6 November, at Belle Vue, they performed Verdi's *Requiem* in her memory, with the rain beating on the roof. The soloists were Sylvia Fisher, Constance Shacklock, Franz Lechleitner and Tom Williams. A preface to the programme, by Barbirolli, referred to 'this fiery young spirit, in whose frame quivered the very essence of musical beauty and nobility'. Barbirolli also this season conducted Bax's *The Tale the Pine Trees Knew*, Strauss's *Metamorphosen* (in memory of the composer, who had died a month earlier), Ponce's Guitar Concerto (with Segovia), Poulenc's Double Piano Concerto, Berkeley's *Four Poems of St Teresa of Avila*, with Ferrier as soloist, Reger's *Variations and Fugue on a Theme of Mozart*, Elgar's First Symphony (four days after Barbirolli's fiftieth birthday), Maurice Johnstone's rhapsody *Tarn Hows*, Walton's Violin Concerto (Grinke), the first Manchester performances of Bartók's *Concerto for Orchestra* and Ireland's *Satyricon* overture, Mozart's *Serenata Notturna*, Alwyn's Oboe Concerto, Strauss's *Till Eulenspiegel* and *Tod und Verklärung*, Rubbra's Fifth Symphony, Dvořák's Cello Concerto (Pierre Fournier), three items from Mozart's *Idomeneo* in Busoni's arrangement, and Ibert's Flute Concerto (Oliver Bannister). He put Vaughan Williams's Sixth Symphony into a Belle Vue programme and of course he conducted such favourites as Berlioz's *Symphonie Fantastique* and Schubert's Great C major Symphony. In those days the season ended with the Pension Fund concert. For it on 14 May, the Hallé combined with the B.B.C. Northern Orchestra at Belle Vue for Strauss's *Ein Heldenleben*, its first Hallé performance since 1938 and the first time Barbirolli conducted it. It was preceded by his presentation of six twenty-year service medals to players who included Wallace Jones and Philip Hecht.

The guest conductors in 1949-50 included Sargent, Krips, Igor Markevitch (who later contributed an article to the *Hallé* magazine in which he paid tribute to the orchestra's 'extremely civilised mentality and great sense of responsibility'), Bernard Herrmann (Liszt's *Faust Symphony* without the choral ending), Hugo Rignold, Previtali (Cherubini's Symphony and an extract from Zandonai's *Romeo and Juliet*), and the Boyd Neel Orchestra, who gave the first Hallé performance of Britten's *Variations on a Theme by Frank Bridge* and revived Bliss's *Music for Strings*. Bliss's *Morning Heroes* was conducted by Bardgett, with Sir Ralph Richardson as narrator. During Bardgett's régime with the choir, one did not need to be reminded that 'let's hear choral' is an anagram of Hallé Orchestra! Among the soloists were the violinists Gioconda de Vito, Ida Haendel, Jean Pougnet and the pianists Claudio Arrau (Schumann with Barbirolli), James Gibb, Edwin Fischer (Mozart No. 22 in E flat, K. 482, with Barbirolli, who said afterwards 'He was wonderful, but I never quite knew when he was coming back to us in the cadenzas'), Cyril Smith, Monique Haas, Livia Rev, Josef Weingarten, Denis Matthews and Eileen Joyce (who played Mozart's 27th concerto and Falla's *Nights in the Gardens of Spain* at Belle Vue with Barbirolli).

The 1950-1 season was the last at the Albert Hall and began with a work the Hallé had introduced at the 1950 Cheltenham Festival, Bax's Piano Concerto for left hand, written after the soloist Harriet Cohen had injured her other hand. Barbirolli's enterprising programme-building continued. He conducted Ibert's *Escales*, Roussel's Third Symphony, Sibelius's *King Christian* suite, Schumann's Cello Concerto (the soloist, Joseph Schuster, had been his principal in New York), Turina's *Fantastic Dances*, Vaughan Williams's Fourth Symphony (its first Manchester performances on 22 and 23 November), the first Hallé performance of Mozart's Serenade in C minor for wind instruments (K. 388), Dukas's *La Péri*, the first Manchester performance of Chausson's *Poème de l'amour et de la mer*, with Ferrier as soloist (it was of this performance that Bernard Herrmann remarked that 'it was like living in sin with Kathleen'!), a concert performance of Gluck's *Orfeo* (at Belle Vue) with Ferrier, Ena Mitchell and Fulvia Trevisani, the first Hallé performance of Ravel's G major Piano Concerto (Monique Haas) and of Stravinsky's *Symphony in Three Movements*, the Love Scene from Strauss's *Feuersnot*, and concertos for two pianos by Bach and Martinu, with Ethel Bartlett and Rae Robertson.

It was a good season for Britten. On 5 November at Belle Vue, Bardgett conducted the *Spring Symphony*, with Joan Cross, Anne Wood and Peter Pears (the work was barely a year old) and on 31 January Paul Kletzki's Albert Hall programme included the *Serenade* with Pears and Dennis Brain as tenor and horn soloists. Tippett's Double String Concerto was introduced to Manchester by Charles Groves on 20 and 21 December, Hans Schmidt-Isserstedt conducted Bruckner's Third Symphony (not heard at the Hallé since 1913) and Kletzki's performance of Mahler's Fourth was heralded by an article by Cardus in the *Hallé* magazine, issued monthly at this period and now a collector's item. The Boyd Neel Orchestra spread all the Brandenburg Concertos over two evenings at the Albert Hall. In the second half of the season, several extra guest conductors took the place of the convalescing Barbirolli. They included Walter Süsskind, Hugo Rignold (with Raymond Cohen as soloist in Elgar's Violin Concerto), Rudolf

Schwarz, Sargent, Albert Wolff, and Ernest Ansermet, who conducted Bartók's *Concerto for Orchestra* and, in one programme, Mozart's last three symphonies. The Hallé's last performance in the Albert Hall was of Brahms's Second Symphony, conducted by Barbirolli. It was preceded by Mozart's Sinfonia Concertante, with Laurance Turner and George Alexander as violin and viola soloists. To glance at the lists of the orchestral players at this juncture is to remind oneself of famous names and old friends: Jane Marcus, Eric Davis, Elizabeth Richardson, Audrey Napier-Smith, Sydney Partington, Gertrude Barker, Norah Winstanley and Phyllis Greenhalgh in the violins; Sydney Errington, William Huddart, Frank Park and Donald Shepherd in the violas; Harold Beck, Paul Ward, Gladys Yates, Sydney Wright, Alexander Ferrier, Norah Sandeman in the cellos; Arthur Shaw and Richard Tildesley leading the basses; Janet Craxton, Patricia Stancliffe and Michael Winfield the oboe section; Pat Ryan and Leonard Regan, clarinets; Charles Cracknell and Bert Mitton among the bassoonists; the horns led by Maurice Handford, with Arthur Bevan and Enid Roper; Sydney King principal trumpet; Maisie Ringham principal trombone, with Terence Nagle and Norman Beattie; Wally Jones on tuba, Joyce Aldous the timpanist, and a percussion section of Leslie Newland, Rayson Whalley and Tom Cheetham.

x—*Towards the centenary*

Although the Hallé, after November 1951, was back in its traditional but modernised home, the Free Trade Hall did not solve many problems. It belongs to Manchester Corporation and is not exclusively a concert-hall. The corporation hires out the hall and the Hallé is merely one of many customers. Compare this with the Liverpool Philharmonic Hall, where the orchestra holds all its rehearsals and the administrative staff has its offices, all for a very moderate fee. The Hallé in 1951 still rehearsed in the cramped room at the top of a disused Victorian school in Hewitt Street, near Central Station, which had served them since just after Barbirolli's arrival.

The 1950-1 season had brought in receipts of nearly £100,000, the largest in the Hallé's history hitherto, but the deficit was still £7,664, most of which was met by Manchester Corporation. By January 1952 a new financial crisis occurred. For its first Free Trade Hall season, the Society reverted to twenty-two weekly Thursday concerts, with eighteen on Sundays, five on Saturdays and four miscellaneous events at Belle Vue. In addition, the orchestra was increased to eighty-eight players. The hall seated 2,500, in contrast to the 3,700 accommodated at the two successive Albert Hall evenings. Many Society members complained they could not get Thursday seats. Godlee announced an impending deficit of £17,000, and gave a warning of a ten per cent cut in the orchestra's salaries. Crickmore's first task, ironically, was to prune the administrative staff. He realised the seat prices in the Free Trade Hall had been fixed too low but could not be altered for a year. So he had to find other sources of revenue. He launched a summer series of popular Promenade Concerts and a series of industrial concerts, such as had proved successful in Liverpool and Birmingham, at which firms and factories were offered block bookings at reduced prices. Rehearsal costs were kept low because the same programme was repeated on two or three nights and perhaps also played in another town. George Weldon (1908-63), conductor of the City of Birmingham Symphony Orchestra from 1943 to 1951, was appointed associate conductor in charge of these new ventures, which meant an increase from 205 to 235 concerts a year. Crickmore also decided to revert for the 1952-3 season to fortnightly mid-week concerts at the Free Trade Hall and a return to Belle Vue. Having put the Hallé's house in order, he then awaited the results of his pleas to the city council to abandon the guarantee-against-loss system which Bean had favoured and to make a direct grant so that the Society could budget ahead. In July 1952, the city council voted to give the Hallé £9,000 a year for the next three years. Alderman Richard Harper pointed out, to his credit, that this was not as generous as it looked because the corporation recouped £7,000 a year in rent for the Free Trade Hall. But at least the Society knew where it stood, and there is no doubt that Crickmore saved the Hallé from bankruptcy at this juncture. The Belle Vue decision was welcomed, but as the Free Trade Hall habit grew, audiences proved less willing to go to Longsight. A Hallé generation, however, has affectionate memories of the Belle Vue atmosphere. Big though the hall was, there was an intimate atmosphere, probably because the orchestra played in the centre (the circus ring) with the audience all round it. Sometimes rain on the roof 'drowned' the music, sometimes birds sang in the roof, sometimes animal noises from the zoo penetrated the silences, but it was all enjoyable.

On 27 September 1952, four days before the opening of the 95th Manchester season, Philip Godlee died suddenly, aged 62. His 1914-18 war wounds had killed him at last. He had been chairman for nearly ten years; he had transformed the orchestra's working schedule and its national standing; he had found and retained a great conductor; and he had seen the Society's membership increase in a decade from below one hundred to over 1,800. Barbirolli was stricken; he gave the memorial address in St Ann's Church, Manchester, on 1 October, referring to Godlee as 'that gay, courageous and noble spirit . . . His sudden and untimely passing leaves a great gap in my heart and in my musical life amongst you. From the day of my arrival in Manchester, we seemed to find an affinity of spirit, identity of purpose and source of mutual trust.' That evening, he conducted Elgar's Second Symphony in memory of his friend, the music of mingled joy and sorrow, joy for a rich and enriching life, sorrow for the end of a Hallé era. On his death-bed, Godlee had said: 'Don't let Leonard be chairman', but it was Behrens who succeeded him, a choice inevitable both by reason of seniority and family association. He at once wrote to Barbirolli: 'We have disagreed in the past and we may disagree again, but nothing can ever extinguish in my mind my gratitude to you and my admiration for the immortal (that is the right word) services you have rendered to all of us.' Behrens and Barbirolli were personally antipathetic – and, after Godlee, no chairman would have had easy acceptance from Barbirolli – but Behrens was a genuine admirer of his conductor as a musician and said on more than one occasion 'I could never accept the responsibility of harming the man who *is* the Hallé'. Suspicious at first of Crickmore, he came to admire his business acumen. At the Society's meeting in December 1952, Behrens reported that the expected deficit of £17,000 had been reduced to an actual loss of £3,035. Grants had increased by £3,672 and 209 concerts had been given.

The month of November 1952 saw the Hallé's first appearances on the new long-playing gramophone records and on television. In June and July 1953 the orchestra went abroad for the first time for nearly three years, giving fourteen concerts in fourteen days in Bulawayo, Rhodesia (now Zimbabwe). This was part of the Cecil Rhodes centenary festival. Bulawayo had never before had symphony concerts and nearly thirty thousand people attended during the fortnight. Among the music played was Berlioz's *Symphonie fantastique*, Ravel's *Daphnis and Chloë*, Vaughan Williams's *Sinfonia Antartica* and symphonies by Beethoven, Brahms and Sibelius. Increased salaries for the players during 1953 led to a conference to give effect to Bean's 1949 idea for regional support of the Hallé and Liverpool Philharmonic. Only forty-three of 153 councils showed any interest, agreeing to guarantee £21,328 to the two orchestras for 1954-5 and 1955-6. The average contribution was £350, Manchester's being £5,991. In 1952-3 the Hallé made a profit of £5,451 on 243 concerts; in 1953-4 a profit of

£15,067 on 264 concerts; and in 1954-5 a loss of £1,098 on 255 concerts. The reason for the variation between 1953-4 and the following year was that Manchester's three-year £9,000 grant expired in 1953-4 and the Arts Council reduced its grant by £3,000 in 1954-5. The Hallé felt that its success in paying its way (its box-office revenue was higher than that of any other British orchestra) had led to its penalisation by the Arts Council. Barbirolli remained extremely disgruntled because the Liverpool Philharmonic's policy of playing concerts of avant-garde music attracted a larger Arts Council grant even though it attracted only small audiences. Because of its financial economies, the Hallé was at this time the object of much criticism on the grounds of unenterprising programmes, second-rate soloists and fewer guest conductors. Crickmore explored a new source of revenue when in 1955 he signed a three-year contract with the commercial television company Associated Rediffusion for fortnightly Hallé appearances. He also obtained an option on Barbirolli's services until at least the end of the 1957-8 season (the orchestra's hundredth). In October 1955, the orchestra gave one concert in Paris. Barbirolli was still disappointed that the committee were not fulfilling their 1948 promise of an annual foreign tour, but hopes of a tour of the United States in the centenary season sustained him.

The announcement in March 1956 that this American tour would not materialise because of the lack of £15,000 for fares precipitated the next crisis. Barbirolli took this deeply to heart. In 1955 the Hallé committee had set aside £3,000 of the reserve fund for the centenary season and they offered this sum for a foreign tour. Barbirolli told Crickmore in April 1956 that it was inadequate and explained why: 'The reserves constantly referred to have really been created by the sacrifices I have made for many years now by conducting for fees well below those paid to guest conductors and by my non-insistence on the fulfilment of the promises made me by the general committee, which included the three corporation representatives, when I refused the B.B.C. offer in 1948 . . . If I am right in remembering Bean at that time budgeted £3,000 a year for foreign tours [this was the minimum figure suggested by Bean], of which I think only £3,000 has been spent, there is £21,000 of what I might call my reserves. I now conduct Hallé concerts at one-third of the fee paid me for my other concerts in this country and for one-quarter of the fees paid me abroad . . . For some years I have played with fewer members in the orchestra than was promised me, and this has effected a saving, I am informed by you, amounting to not less than £3,000 a year. Between this and the discrepancy in the fees paid to guests, it should be clearly seen that I have, in fact, presented the Society with the sum of about £6,000 a year . . . All these sacrifices I have made so that the orchestra should have their rightful place in the international scene, but if this is not to be, then I do feel that the time has come for me to be sensible and at least ask that the average guest conductor fee be paid to me also, though I am willing for this to go in the foreign tour pool if this money is earmarked for that purpose.' Barbirolli wanted the committee also to publicise the facts on Manchester's grant to the Hallé compared with what other cities gave. The figures he supplied to them showed that Birmingham gave £25,000, Liverpool £17,000, Glasgow £15,815, Leeds £10,000 (despite the disbanding of the Yorkshire Symphony Orchestra in 1955), Sheffield £6,000 – and Manchester £9,000, less £7,044 rent for the hall, a total of £1,956.

Within a fortnight matters came to a head. Barbirolli told the committee he would not consider the 1956-7 programmes nor the centenary season until he had settled the future financing of the orchestra in relation to its huge prestige. He sent them proposals for his contract from August 1956 to July 1960 'as at present, with the exception of the following revision: either (a) a fee of £100 per concert or (b) present salary and expenses (approx. £6,000 per annum for 120 concerts) but a sub-clause to provide that the Society would negotiate for approximately fourteen days of foreign engagements for the orchestra in each year, with a guaranteed minimum of eight days per year, it being understood that an average of £6,000 per annum (i.e. approx. remainder of Sir John's new fee of £100 per concert × 120 concerts) be available for subsidising such engagements. Any residue at July 1960 from the total four-year pool of £24,000 to revert to the Society.' Even at £100, Barbirolli was giving the Hallé a bargain, for his fee to other organisations at that date was 150 guineas. The committee agreed to (b).

At the same time, concerned as ever over the loss of some of his best players to London and other orchestras, Barbirolli implored Crickmore to obtain better rates of pay for principals. The B.B.C. was paying £17 5s to its rank-and-file, which was £1 5s more than the Hallé basic rate for principals. He urged a 'ceiling' for principals of £30, adding: 'You have become used to being tailored by Savile Row at Burton prices. I will help you to retain this illusion as long as I can, but cannot guarantee to do so until further notice.' He pointed out that some of those who had left had come to the Hallé 'merely as just good instrumentalists, with practically no experience whatsoever . . . To offset the difficulty of having sufficient rehearsal time to give them their full training in the orchestra, many of them spent hours with me at my flat, where I gave them private tuition. It is surely too much to expect that I should have to start doing this all over again. I tell you quite frankly, Ken, that I could not possibly do this, if only from physical reasons.'

The 'physical reasons' were obvious to everyone in the summer of 1956. He looked ill and was often in pain. It was no surprise when in August he had a serious abdominal operation and was ordered a complete rest until the end of the year. Enforced idleness always accentuated the chronic depression which afflicted him throughout his life and he fought against it by preparatory work on the scores of Bach's *St Matthew Passion* and Bruckner's Seventh and Mahler's Second Symphonies. Before his operation, the doctor had noticed that the heart 'murmur' he had had since birth was more in evidence. 'The warning from the old "ticker" must perforce be taken notice of', Barbirolli wrote to a friend. Henceforward he was rarely to be free from pain to the end of his life: stones in the kidneys caused him severe backache and his heart ailment grew steadily worse. Yet he was physically dauntless and never spared himself.

He interrupted his convalescence in Italy in November 1956 to return to Manchester when it seemed that lack of money would jeopardise the centenary plans. He addressed a private meeting of the city council, pointing out that the Hallé's reward for giving 238 concerts in the 1955-6 season had been a cut in the Arts Council grant 'and Manchester Corporation's contribution apart from the regional scheme was nil . . . Why, for being such good and honest custodians of the public moneys entrusted to us, do we have to be punished in this way?' He quoted to them the comparisons with other cities given above and ended: 'Can you examine your consciences and feel that all has been done that could have been done?' The result was a special additional grant of £5,298 towards the cost of the hundredth season.

The programmes of the centenary season will be described in their place. The centenary concert itself, on 30 January 1958, was attended by the Princess Royal and the Earl and Countess of Harewood, and by Charles Hallé's granddaughter, Mlle. Cécile Sartoris. The first half of the concert was televised by the B.B.C. and when Barbirolli walked to the rostrum the whole audience rose to cheer him. The programme opened with the *Freischütz* overture, Hallé's choice a century before. Then Clifford Curzon, survivor of the pianists Barbirolli had 'sacked' on his arrival in 1943, was soloist in Brahms's B flat concerto, which Hallé had played in 1882 when it was new. The symphony was Elgar's First, born at a Hallé concert nearly fifty years earlier. In the *Manchester Guardian*, Colin Mason wrote that the Elgar performance was 'not four movements, but a single symphonic-poem . . . It may be doubted whether Richter himself did better for the work than this.' Towards the end of the season Barbirolli announced that he would henceforward be conductor-in-chief, not permanent conductor, and would reduce his Hallé commitments to about seventy concerts a year, so that he could accept the engagements with foreign orchestras (including, to his special pleasure, the New York Philharmonic) which he had for so long refused. In March 1958 he was given the honorary freedom of Manchester. 'I have no intention of leaving Hallé,' he told the Town Hall audience, 'for my heart is ever with my children of the orchestra and the people of this great city.'

The season's climax was a tour of Europe. In 1957 the orchestra had given concerts at Ravello, in Italy. Now it opened what was then its most extensive tour with a concert in Hallé's birthplace, Hagen. Other concerts were given in Prague, Warsaw and Linz. Music by Elgar and Vaughan Williams was featured, and in Linz, the composer's birthplace, they played Bruckner's Fourth Symphony. For Barbirolli, the tour was overshadowed by the absence of Crickmore, who had had a leg amputated after the discovery that he had cancer.

Of the orchestra which Barbirolli re-created in 1943, only fourteen players remained in 1958. Two more stalwarts retired at the end of the centenary season: Laurance Turner, leader since 1939, and Pat Ryan, principal clarinet, who had played under Harty. In 1958, too, Charles Collier, harpist in Richter's time and in Barbirolli's, died at the age of eighty-six, having retired in 1948 (though he had played occasionally thereafter). Turner was succeeded by a thirty-year-old Lancastrian, Martin Milner, and Ryan by Keith Puddy. Thus the Hallé entered its second century.

XI—*The music, 1951-8*

Notwithstanding the euphoria of the re-opening of the Free Trade Hall, it should not be thought that there were no critical voices among the Hallé's adoring audience. A review by one P.J.C. in the periodical *Music Survey* (vol. II, No. 4, spring 1950, p. 277) referred to the orchestra as 'an adequate playing mechanism but like most of the major English orchestras it lacks the stature and a conductor really worthy of its musicianship . . . The orchestra has been most successful in music where blatancy in performance is not a vice but a virtue. That the Hallé is developing two tones, the harsh and the sentimental, is a pity.' The gibe at Barbirolli was described in the next issue as 'bunk and mischievous bunk at that' by Geoffrey Sharp, editor of *The Music Review*, while the joint editor of *Music Survey*, Hans Keller, somewhat unchivalrously if right-mindedly described his contributor's notice as 'quite incompetent'. The contributor's defence was to attack Barbirolli's 'careless phrasing, tendencies towards sentimentality and lack of an integrating perspective of a work's organic development, symmetry and meaning'. He perhaps gave his real game away when he added: 'Give the Hallé a Beecham . . . and all would be more than well'. Echoes of 1944? Perhaps more interesting were the views of Paul Kletzki after his first encounter with the Hallé. He told the Press in January 1951 that he was 'speechless' when he considered the standards reached by the orchestra in spite of their working conditions. He thought two hundred concerts a year 'far too many . . . I am amazed to see them after a concert, say, in Harrogate finishing at 9.45 p.m. travel home in a motor coach for three hours in bad weather and then arrive for rehearsal next morning as fresh as flowers. It is heroic.' In the Hewitt Street rehearsal room he had seen Hallé players 'with woollen gloves on, just as I saw the French orchestras in 1945'.

With the end of the Albert Hall era, there was a change of music critic on the *Manchester Guardian*, as it was still called. The urbane Granville Hill, with pince-nez, sombre suit and a quiet wit, retired and was replaced by the twenty-seven-year-old Colin Mason, who had no previous Manchester connections and intensely disliked the place. (The *Daily Telegraph* had also just appointed a new young Manchester critic.) Mason made a stir with his notice of the Belle Vue Beethoven concert which opened the 1951-2 season. He was not impressed by the King's Hall acoustics and he thought the performances rather ordinary. Although in the next few years he wrote many appreciative notices of the Hallé, somehow he never overcame the impression of hostility conveyed by that first and very mild criticism. He was a most perceptive, indeed a great critic, who died far too young.

There were three Belle Vue concerts before the inaugural festival in the Free Trade Hall. In a ballet programme Barbirolli conducted Walton's Bach transcriptions *The Wise Virgins* and Walter Süsskind conducted the first Hallé performance of Tchaikovsky's Second Symphony. When the season proper of weekly Thursday concerts began in the new hall, the connecting thread was the series of symphonies – then numbering six – by Vaughan Williams to anticipate the celebration of his eightieth birthday in October 1952. The *London* and Brahms's First Symphony were played at the first concert on 29 November. Mason wrote that the orchestra played 'as near flawlessly as any conductor could wish, as fully realising Barbirolli's intentions as he the composers''. The composer himself conducted *A Sea Symphony* in Manchester and Sheffield on 20 and 21 March 1952, with Barbirolli playing at the first desk of cellos in Sheffield. The soloists were Isobel Baillie and Denis Dowling. Other features of the season were the performances of five symphonies by Haydn, with whom Barbirolli generally had more affinity, five by Schubert and six by Mozart, including a repeat of the programme comprising Nos. 39, 40 and 41 which Barbirolli had had to yield to Ansermet because of illness, and a complementary evening at which Barbirolli conducted Nos. 34, 35 and 36. Sir John also conducted *Messiah* for the first time, in Sheffield (8 December 1951) and Manchester, restoring certain features of the original scoring. The soloists at the Manchester performance on 13 April 1952 were Elisabeth Schwarzkopf, Kathleen Ferrier, William Herbert and Hervey Alan. Ferrier was also heard as the Angel in *Gerontius*, on 24 April in Mahler's *Das Lied von der Erde*, her tenor partner in both these works being Richard Lewis, and in Brahms's *Alto Rhapsody*. Other works Barbirolli conducted were the complete Falla *El Amor Brujo*, with Marina de Gabarain as mezzo soloist, the (surprisingly) first Hallé performance of Strauss's First Horn Concerto (Maurice Handford), Britten's *Sinfonia da Requiem*, a Wagner evening with Sylvia Fisher and Ludwig Suthaus (singers with whom he was working at Covent Garden at this time), Ravel's *Shéhérazade* (Janine Micheau) and Act 2 of *Aida*.

Guest conductors were Sargent, who conducted the Christmas *Messiah* at Belle Vue, Previtali (Busoni's *Tanz-Walzer*), Albert Wolff, Schmidt-Isserstedt (Egk's *French Suite*), Boult (with the L.P.O., to give the first Manchester performance of Mahler's *Lieder eines fahrenden Gesellen*, soloist Eugenia Zareska, on 7 February, the day after the death of King George VI), and Kletzki, who conducted Petrassi's *Concerto for Orchestra* and Bruckner's Seventh Symphony. Among the season's soloists were the violinists Carmel Hakendorf, Raymond Cohen, Jacques Thibaud, and Endre Wolf; the pianists Julius Katchen, Valda Aveling, Gina Bachauer, Moura Lympany and Cyril Smith; and the cellists Antonio Janigro and André Navarra. The latter played Haydn's D major concerto in an edition by Barbirolli.

For 1952-3 the midweek series reverted to a repeated programme on Wednesday and Thursday. It opened with an Elgar programme which included the Second Symphony played in memory of Godlee. Later in the season Raymond Cohen played the Violin Concerto. All Beethoven's and Brahms's symphonies were performed, four of Beethoven's piano concertos and the Violin Concerto, and three of

73

Brahms's four works in concerto form. The principal novelty was the first performance, on 14 January 1953, of Vaughan Williams's *Sinfonia Antartica*, a further result of the friendship between the composer and the Hallé and its conductor, whom he dubbed 'Glorious John'. Other unfamiliar works performed were Bax's Sixth Symphony, Hindemith's *Symphonic Metamorphosis of Themes by Weber*, Alwyn's *The Magic Island*, Jean Françaix's *Les Bosquets de Cythère* (its first English performance), Moeran's *Serenade*, Ravel's left-hand Piano Concerto (soloist Robert Casadesus), Howells's *Hymnus Paradisi* (conducted by Bardgett), Guarnieri's Second Symphony (conducted by George Weldon), Nielsen's Fourth Symphony (Weldon) and Violin Concerto (Henry Holst, Barbirolli), and John Gardner's *Variations on a Waltz by Nielsen*. Kathleen Ferrier was the soloist in Brahms's *Four Serious Songs* (in Sargent's orchestration) in October and sang in the Christmas *Messiah* at Belle Vue on 7 December. These were her last Manchester appearances, for she was already dying of cancer. For the Easter performances of *Messiah* and *Gerontius* her place was taken by, respectively, Kathleen Joyce and Constance Shacklock. Guest conductors included Vittorio Gui, Pierre Monteux (*La Mer*) and the Australian Sir Bernard Heinze (Shostakovich's Fifth Symphony), while the Philharmonia Orchestra, conducted by Richard Austin, played in Manchester on 26 October 1952.

Two musicians who had visited Manchester during the 1952-3 season died in the opening weeks of the 1953-4 season, Kathleen Ferrier and Arnold Bax. In memory of the singer he adored, Barbirolli conducted Delius's *Idyll*, Elgar's Prelude to *Gerontius* and *Enigma Variations*, and Fauré's *Requiem*, while for the composer he had known for so many years he conducted the left-hand Piano Concerto, with Harriet Cohen, and the Fifth Symphony. The Bax symphony was new to these concerts, and so were the Delius *Idyll* and his Cello Concerto, which the Hallé's principal cellist Harold Beck played on 8 November. At the first concert on 14 October, Barbirolli conducted the first performance of Alwyn's Second Symphony and, on 27 January, the first Manchester performance of Wordsworth's Third Symphony. He repeated Vaughan Williams's *Sinfonia Antartica* and introduced Chagrin's *Lamento Appassionato*, a suite from Strauss's opera *Die Liebe der Danae*, Lennox Berkeley's Piano Concerto and Fauré's *La bonne chanson* (with Richard Lewis). But his principal achievements were the first Manchester performance since 1930 of Mahler's Ninth Symphony on 24 February 1954 and the first in the city of Berg's Violin Concerto, with André Gertler, on 21 April. The Mahler was introduced by Cardus, who somewhat unflatteringly likened it to 'a kind of musical toothache'. The symphony was first played on 19 February in Bradford and later in Sheffield, London, Edinburgh and other cities. Where Harty had been limited to perhaps five hours of rehearsal for this complex and difficult work, Barbirolli had nearly fifty. The result showed in a most impressive performance. Both the Mahler and the Berg were repeated in the 1954-5 season. In his second season as associate conductor in 1953-4, George Weldon conducted Walton's Symphony and Elgar's *The Music Makers* (solo contralto Gladys Ripley, who was also to die from cancer in 1955). Schmidt-Isserstedt, Kletzki and Previtali were again the chief guest conductors.

The 1954-5 programmes were less enterprising, with a big Brahms and Beethoven bias. Nevertheless several works catch the eye, for example Samuel Barber's First Symphony, Elgar's *In the South* (not performed since 1922), Walton's *Belshazzar's Feast*, Bliss's Piano Concerto (Clive Lythgoe), Rawsthorne's *Symphonic Studies*, Delius's *Cynara* (first Manchester performance, with John Cameron, baritone). Donatoni's Timpani Concertino (Joyce Aldous), Vaughan Williams's *Job* and Tuba Concerto, all conducted by George Weldon. Barbirolli conducted Bliss's *Music for Strings*, Villa-Lobos's *Bachianas Brasileiras No. 4*, Delius's *Song of the High Hills*, Fauré's *Ballade* (pianist Marie-Thérèse Fourneau) – this had not been played since 1925 at the Hallé – Ravel's *Shéhérazade* and Milhaud's *Chansons de Ronsard*, both with Janine Micheau, Ibert's *Le chevalier errant*, Rubbra's Sixth Symphony, Elgar's Violin Concerto, several works by Strauss including the Waltz Scene from *Intermezzo*, the prelude to *Capriccio*, and the *Four Last Songs* (Elisabeth Schwarzkopf), all first Manchester performances, Khatchaturyan's Cello Concerto (Henri Honegger), and many of Sir John's favourite works (*La Mer*, Dvořák's Seventh, *Gerontius* and *Messiah*). On 3 and 4 November he preceded Elgar's *Falstaff* with a lengthy spoken analysis during which the orchestra illustrated his talk with over forty music examples. Colin Mason's comments on the Rubbra Symphony are worth preserving: 'There is a welcome delight in sheer beauty, colour and variety of orchestral sound that has been rare, and lacking, in his music. Most important, there is a brightness and gaiety almost unknown in the symphonies of the last twenty-five years. It is in this that Rubbra shows himself, in spite of the increasing conservatism of his language, one of the genuinely progressive composers of his generation.'

In the guest conductors' programmes, Georges Tzipine conducted works by Tailleferre and Auric (*Phèdre*), and brought a brilliant pianist, Samson François, to play Prokofiev's third concerto. It was a good season for women pianists – Gina Bachauer, Eileen Joyce, Phyllis

Sellick and Moura Lympany among them. Khatchaturyan conducted his own *Three Dances from Gayaneh* and at the Pension Fund concert the Clayton Aniline Works Band gave the first Hallé performance of Elgar's *Severn Suite*.

The 1955-6 season won few laurels from advocates of adventure. Once again, Brahms was the foundation of the programmes, with performances of all the symphonies, overtures and concertos – and the *German Requiem*, which had not been performed at these concerts since February 1931. On 30 November 1955 the soloists, with the Hallé Choir, were Hilde Zadek (soprano) and Otakar Kraus (baritone). Barbirolli conducted. All the Tchaikovsky symphonies, including *Manfred*, were also performed, with the first two piano concertos (No. 2 had not been played since 1886, when Hallé was soloist), the Violin Concerto and other works. (The First Symphony was receiving its first Hallé performance when Weldon conducted it on 27 November.) Beethoven and Mozart were also strongly represented. Another first Hallé performance under Weldon was that of Haydn's Symphony No. 31 (the 'Horn Signal') on 7 March 1956. Contemporary works included a Sibelius programme for the composer's ninetieth birthday, a second performance of Rubbra's Sixth Symphony, a suite from Lennox Berkeley's opera *Nelson*, Bliss's scena *The Enchantress*, sung by Pamela Bowden, the first Manchester performance of Britten's *Scottish Ballad* for two pianos (Gorini and Lorenzi, with Barbirolli conducting) and the Jugoslav composer Stjepan Sulek's Second Symphony (Weldon). Barbirolli conducted the first Manchester performances of Hindemith's Piano Concerto (Adolph Hallis), Stravinsky's *Symphony of Psalms*, and, with Richard Lewis as solo tenor, the orchestral version of Vaughan Williams's *On Wenlock Edge*. This was a prelude to the big event of the season, the first performance on 2 May of the Eighth Symphony by Vaughan Williams which was dedicated to Barbirolli. The composer, now eighty-three, attended the rehearsals and performance. On 18 March he had himself conducted the Hallé in Bach's *St Matthew Passion*, its first Hallé performance since 1904 and a memorable one.

Two other memorable events had occurred in November 1955. At the midweek concerts on the 2nd and 3rd, Beecham at last returned to the Hallé series, with his Royal Philharmonic Orchestra. His performance of the national anthem, Colin Mason remarked, 'would have quelled a rebellion' and it was followed by marvellous accounts of Berlioz, Mozart ('Prague' Symphony), Delius and Tchaikovsky (*Manfred*, its first Hallé performance since March 1904). The audience was ecstatic. A fortnight later Barbirolli conducted Mahler's First

Symphony, not played in Manchester since Balling's 1913 performance. To quote Mason again: 'The orchestra played like an immense chamber orchestra, all soloists yet completely at one under the conductor, they giving every detail of the score its proper colour while he made the colours into a composition.' If ever there was proof of the effectiveness of competitive rivalry, this was it! During this season Tzipine conducted the first performance in England of the Symphony in F by Gossec (1734-1829), Clara Haskil was soloist in Chopin's F minor concerto with Barbirolli, and Malcuzynski played Rachmaninov's third concerto with Weldon. Barbirolli conducted the 'Nimrod' variation of Elgar in memory of John F. Russell, writer of the Hallé programme-notes for many years and former librarian of the Henry Watson Music Library in Manchester, who died in March.

Because of his convalescence, Barbirolli missed the opening concerts of the 1956–7 season. Weldon, therefore, conducted the first Elgar work in the season, *Falstaff*, part of a major celebration to herald the composer's centenary on 2 June 1957. Barbirolli returned for *Messiah* on 9 December and three days later commemorated the fiftieth anniversary of Richter's death (5 December 1916) with Elgar's *Elegy*. At the same concert he conducted Rubbra's Piano Concerto (Iso Elinson). The principal Elgar concerts were on 1 May (*Introduction and Allegro*, Cello Concerto, with André Navarra, and Second Symphony), *The Dream of Gerontius* on the hundredth birthday, 2 June (Constance Shacklock, Ronald Dowd and Nowakowski), and the three chamber works on 7 May, with Barbirolli as cellist with Laurance Turner, Sydney Partington, Rachel Godlee, and Wilfrid Parry (piano) in the String Quartet and Piano Quintet, and the sonata played by Carmel Hakendorf and Parry. David Willcocks conducted the first Hallé performance of *The Apostles* since March 1926 on 17 March 1957. The soloists were Ena Mitchell, Pamela Bowden, Ronald Bristol, Hervey Alan, John Cameron and John Carol Case. The audience was deplorably small. After one of the Hallé's London performances this year, Neville Cardus wrote: 'Sir John and the Hallé serve Elgar as once on a time the Vienna Philharmonic and Bruno Walter served Bruckner.'

But it was not all Elgar. Barbirolli repeated Mahler's First and Vaughan Williams's Eighth Symphonies, conducted Bruckner's Seventh and the first Manchester performances of Nielsen's *Maskarade* overture (9 January 1957) and Fifth Symphony (6 February), Rachmaninov's Third Symphony, Mahler's *Das Lied von der Erde* (Kerstin Meyer and Richard Lewis), the last scene of *Die Walküre* (Sylvia Fisher and Otakar Kraus), Wagner's *Five Wesendonck Songs* (Fisher), a suite from Wolf's *Der Corregidor*, Bloch's Concerto Grosso with piano obbligato (Rayson Whalley), Respighi's *Adagio con variazioni* for cello (Oliver Vella, the Hallé's principal cellist), and a concerto he had arranged from Handel for viola and strings with Sydney Errington, principal viola, as soloist. Tzipine belatedly brought Ravel's *Alborada del gracioso* into the Hallé repertoire and, on 6 March, conducted the first Manchester performance of Shostakovich's Tenth Symphony. Sir Adrian Boult, who had not conducted the Hallé for several years, introduced Finzi's Cello Concerto to Manchester on 31 October 1956, Barbirolli having conducted its first performance with the Hallé at the previous year's Cheltenham Festival. Christopher Bunting was soloist on both occasions. Basil Cameron conducted another Cheltenham work, Iain Hamilton's *Symphonic Variations*, on 17 October, and the first Hallé performance (in the same concert) of Stravinsky's *Pulcinella* suite. Sir Arthur Bliss, Master of the Queen's Music, conducted three of his own works on 16 December, the overture *Edinburgh*, the Violin Concerto (Campoli) and *Morning Heroes*, with Richard Attenborough narrating. The season's other soloists included Monique de la Bruchollerie, Moiseiwitsch, Monique Haas, Edith Fischer, Geza Anda, Samson François, and Gina Bachauer (pianists) and Bronislav Gimpel, Carmel Hakendorf, and Aldo Ferraresi (violinists).

The programmes for the centenary season, 1957-8, were devised by a committee which included Barbirolli, Crickmore and Colin Mason. The last-named strongly urged the inclusion of Tippett's recent Second Symphony, but Barbirolli abandoned it as 'not worth the trouble involved'. Nevertheless a remarkable series of concerts was produced which honoured the past conductors of the orchestra and several major British contemporary composers. Hallé's first concert, 30 January 1858, was repeated on 5 January 1958, with Barbirolli conducting and Weldon taking Hallé's place as pianist in three Mendelssohn *Songs Without Words*. Similarly, on 19 January 1958, Barbirolli reproduced Richter's first Hallé concert of 19 October 1899. Harty was saluted on 9 March with three of his own works, including the tone-poem *With the Wild Geese* and Berlioz's *Symphonie Fantastique*. Lady Harty (Agnes Nicholls) was present. On 4 May Barbirolli conducted his first Bradford programme of 5 July 1943. Hallé was also commemorated on 2 February by a superb performance of Verdi's *Requiem* (Sylvia Fisher, Kerstin Meyer, Richard Lewis and Kim Borg). Britten conducted three of his own works – the *Sea Interludes* from *Peter Grimes*, *Les Illuminations* (Peter Pears) and the Pas de Six from *The Prince of the Pagodas* ballet on 19 March; on 22 January Hindemith conducted his own *Nobilissima Visione* and *Weber Metamorphosis*; Walton on 30

78

April conducted his new *Partita*, the *Portsmouth Point* overture and the Cello Concerto (Erling Bengtsson); and Vaughan Williams, who contributed a *Flourish for Glorious John* for the opening of the season, was accorded an eighty-fifth birthday tribute on 27 October when he was present to hear two of his symphonies, the *London* and No. 8, the *Tallis Fantasia*, the *Wasps* overture and his Coronation arrangement of the 'Old Hundredth'. Among other works conducted by Barbirolli were Bartók's Second Piano Concerto (Andor Foldes), Bax's Violin Concerto (André Gertler), Vivaldi's G minor concerto for violin, strings and organ, Brahms's First Piano Concerto (Artur Rubinstein), Benjamin Dale's Romance for viola, with Lionel Tertis the eighty-one-year-old soloist, Elgar's *The Dream of Gerontius* (the choir being Our Lady's Choral Society, Dublin), Arthur Butterworth's First Symphony, Finzi's *The Fall of the Leaf*, Holst's *The Planets*, an operatic evening of Puccini and Verdi, guitar concertos with Segovia, Rawsthorne's overture *Hallé*, Bruckner's Fourth Symphony, Strauss's *Ein Heldenleben* (combined Hallé and B.B.C. Northern Orchestras), and the first Manchester performance, on 14 May, of Mahler's Second Symphony, with Joan Sutherland, Eugenia Zareska and the Hallé Choir. At long last Stravinsky's *Rite of Spring* was played at a Hallé concert when Herman Lindars conducted it on 27 November with the Royal Philharmonic.

Brief mention only can be made here of other highlights of one of the finest seasons ever given by the Hallé: Claudio Arrau and Barbirolli in the 'Emperor' Concerto, Gina Bachauer and Weldon in Prokofiev's Third Piano Concerto, Moiseiwitsch in Rachmaninov's First Piano Concerto, Myra Hess and Weldon in Beethoven's G major Piano Concerto, Sargent conducting Holst's *The Hymn of Jesus* (its belated first Hallé performance), John Pritchard and the Royal Liverpool Philharmonic in Malcolm Arnold's Third Symphony, Rosalyn Tureck and Hindemith in Bach's D minor keyboard concerto, Jon Vickers as tenor soloist at the Easter performance of *Messiah*, Jascha Horenstein conducting Shostakovich's Fifth Symphony and Schoenberg's *Verklärte Nacht*, and a visit by the Leipzig Gewandhaus Orchestra, conducted by Franz Konwitschny, who played Mozart, Strauss and Schubert (the Great C major).

Naturally, this book concentrates on the Manchester concerts, but many of these programmes were also played in Sheffield, Bradford, London, Leicester and other 'Hallé towns'. The annual tours of the West Country with Barbirolli conducting Elgar, Vaughan Williams and Brahms in the cathedrals, the visits to Scotland and Harrogate, to Bristol, Wolverhampton and many other places were events eagerly anticipated by players and listeners. This was the era when Barbirolli conducted at the annual Hallé Ball at New Year and couples fell in love while they danced to his conducting of Lehár's *Gold and Silver* waltz. Cardus heard the orchestra in London during this centenary season when they played Bruckner's Fourth Symphony. 'Sir John's conducting has the touch of genius', he wrote, 'it is never negative, never non-committal. And the Hallé Orchestra has an unmistakable character. It is a musical community, intent on music-making. It does not perpetually give us the impression as it is playing that it is making a gramophone record.'

Nevertheless it is encouraging to know that because Pye recorded several of the Hallé–Barbirolli performances mentioned above between 1956 and 1961, memory can be checked and heard not to be a delusion.

XII—*J. B.'s last twelve years*

Inevitably, much of the history of the Hallé outside the concert-hall concerns money. It makes for sober and sobering reading, but subsidising the arts is as controversial a topic today as it was a quarter of a century ago. The centenary season ended with a small surplus of £984 instead of the expected £3,000 loss, thanks to special grants from Manchester, the Arts Council and the British Council. Speaking at the annual meeting of the Society in December 1958, Behrens pointed out that, excluding the special centenary grants, out of every pound the Hallé spent, 17s 6d came from their own resources. Ought they to be so little dependent on outside help? he asked. There were orchestras which budgeted for a deficit, confident that when the deficit appeared, rescue would be at hand. 'They may be right. That may be the best way to promote art in this country.' He was, one assumes, being facetious. A year later Behrens retired from the chairmanship, handing over to a Rochdale businessman, Alan Duckworth, a member of the committee since 1936 and the first to hold the office of deputy chairman. The loss in 1958-9 was £4,949, and a pay claim from the orchestra was expected. Incidentally, Behrens stonewalled at the last annual meeting he chaired when a member asked that Beecham should be invited to conduct the Hallé. 'We are always inviting Sir Thomas', he replied.

The Hallé's theme in the 1958–9 report – its *leitmotiv*, one might say – was its resentment at being 'penalised' for its box-office success. The loss of the American tour still rankled. 'We feel', Crickmore (now

O.B.E.) said, 'that if the country can afford subsidies, we as a successful orchestra should get the same subsidy as the other orchestras.' 1960 started encouragingly with an extra £3,000 voted to the Hallé by Manchester City Council, taking the total direct grant back to £9,000, and a new £20,000 contract with Associated Rediffusion for the Hallé to give seventy-eight public concerts in the next three years, with opportunities for young British composers, conductors and soloists. This was good news for the new treasurer, C. Yates Lloyd, who succeeded Lythgoe in February 1960. At the same time there was grumbling in the press and among the audience over the drop in Hallé standards when Barbirolli was away. There were calls for the appointment of a young associate conductor in place of, or in addition to, George Weldon.

When in February 1960 the Government increased its grant to the Arts Council, the Hallé benefited by an overall increase of £7,000 in its Arts Council grant to £22,000. But if Whitehall thought this would pacify Crickmore, they were to be disabused. In May he persuaded Barbirolli, on the eve of his departure to conduct in Budapest, Prague and Israel, to threaten to leave the Hallé at the end of the year unless a general inquiry was made into the subsidies of the principal British orchestras or unless Arts Council subsidies were placed on an equal footing. Barbirolli had harsh words for Manchester Corporation. 'I am sick of being called Manchester's musical ambassador and, when abroad, being told what an asset the Hallé is to its city when I know all the time that Manchester's contribution to the Hallé is so paltry compared with that of other cities to their orchestras. Months ago the Corporation was informed of our plight and of the dangers to the morale of our musicians.'

Barbirolli was particularly concerned about the orchestra's morale at this time. A few days earlier the Musicians' Union had described playing conditions in the Hallé as 'dreadful' and the terms of employment as 'shocking'. Seven players resigned within two weeks. Unrest was also being caused by a former viola player, Malcolm Tillis, who had resigned to write a book about the Hallé, and who went so far as to interrupt the unveiling by the Lord Mayor of a plaque in the Free Trade Hall commemorating two suffragettes. This, Tillis said, was in protest against the 'undemocratic manner' in which the Hallé controlled its affairs.

The Hallé's case against the Arts Council was summed up by figures quoted for the 1958-9 season. The Hallé received £29,181 in local authority and Arts Council grants and took £127,230 at the box-office. The Scottish National Orchestra received £61,915 in grants and took

£37,632 from the public; Liverpool's grants were £50,181, with £71,392 taken in revenue.

When the 103rd season opened, the extra grants awarded, however inequitable they were, had been well spent. Barbirolli now had a complement of thirty-two violins and critics commented favourably on the increased power. A week later he withdrew his threat to leave. The Arts Council's annual report rejected his plea for equal grants, but conceded that 'the present system of subsidising music reveals a certain lack of liaison and unified purpose'. It also showed that the Council's grant of £26,700 to the Hallé for the forthcoming year was almost the equal of those to Birmingham and Liverpool. As one newspaper commented, 'Sir John feels that his point has been taken'. The deficit on this controversial 1959-60 season was £3,318. The committee noted the comments of one of the players who resigned that Hallé programmes were 'routine' compared with Liverpool's Musica Viva series, but refuted the allegations of overwork. The contract with the union allowed a maximum playing time of thirty hours a week, with an average over four weeks of twenty-five hours a week. The average during 1959-60 was twenty-three hours a week, with an average travelling time in the year of nine hours a week. Duckworth contemptuously dismissed suggestions that the Hallé should deliberately run into deficit.

At this time, too, the Hallé ended its regular connection with the Cheltenham Festival of British Contemporary Music, of which it had been the mainstay since 1947, giving four July concerts in each of which a new work was performed. These works were assiduously prepared by Barbirolli for weeks beforehand at no cost to Cheltenham. Over the years, first performances were given of symphonies by Arnell, Fricker, Bate, Benjamin, Wordsworth, John Gardner, Arnold, Simpson, Hamilton and Butterworth and of concertos and smaller pieces by Rawsthorne, Bax, Williamson, Hoddinott, Lennox Berkeley, Whettam, Finzi, Searle, Leighton, Gardner, Seiber, Alwyn, Parrott and Cooke. Each concert ended with a standard-repertory symphony or with a substantial work by Elgar, Vaughan Williams, Bax or Rubbra. The term 'Cheltenham symphony' was coined to describe the result of Barbirolli's predilection for works written in what was then seen as a declining romantic tradition – 'sham antiques' was another pejorative barb. The audiences packed the hall, and there was a real party atmosphere in the Town Hall after each concert as Barbirolli and the players mingled with the festival club members, but some critics and members of the Cheltenham committee grew restive under pressure for programmes in which the rising avant-garde would be represented. Barbirolli was blamed for the lack of enterprise, and there were complaints that, because of his foreign engagements, it was becoming increasingly difficult for him and the other members of the programme selection panel to choose the new works from the many scores submitted. There was also at least one major clash with the panel when Barbirolli refused to conduct a particular work (one of them he described to me as 'liquid manure'). After 1958 the Hallé was gradually phased out of the festival and Barbirolli did not conduct a Cheltenham concert for another seven years. At the 1959 and 1960 festivals it was apparent that the progressives had won the day. Among the new names were Birtwistle, Goehr and Maxwell Davies.

In October 1960 Barbirolli announced that he had accepted an offer by Houston Symphony Orchestra to appoint him conductor-in-chief in succession to Stokowski. This, he said, would not affect his Hallé position. At the same time Crickmore became consultant to the Hallé Society and a member of the committee. He remained Barbirolli's 'attorney'. He was succeeded as general manager by Clive Smart, a twenty-eight-year-old chartered accountant who had been company secretary to the Society under Crickmore's direction since 1958. Smart's first major undertaking was the three-week tour of the Near East in August 1961 during which Barbirolli and the orchestra gave three concerts in the Athens Festival, three in Istanbul, three in Kyrenia, Cyprus, and one at Episcopi for British forces in Cyprus, two in Dubrovnik and one in Turin. He encountered Barbirolli at his most explosive during this tour but the two men established a good working relationship and it is noticeable that once Crickmore had virtually disappeared from the scene, there were fewer dramas and threats to 'resign or else' involving Barbirolli and the Hallé. Not that Barbirolli became acquiescent, but he was more content to leave the management to manage (with continual advice and prodding, of course) and Smart learned to keep his conductor adequately informed on financial and policy matters.

A piquant event on 30 November 1961 should be recorded here. After the Free Trade Hall concert that evening, a bronze bust of Beecham (making him look rather like a Coptic priest) by Ivan Mestrovic was presented to the Society by Granada Television to honour the memory of Sir Thomas, who had died earlier in the year. It was received on behalf of the Hallé by Barbirolli, who said: 'It is fitting that this bust should stand in this hall in which Sir Thomas spent so much time and did so much for music.' Someone said they saw the bust wink, but Sir John did not wink back.

Over the next few years, Manchester and the Arts Council increased their financial aid to the Hallé, although rising salaries and costs eroded each increase almost as soon as it was voted. A significant event, therefore, was the decision by Wilson's Brewery, part of the Watney group, to sponsor a Free Trade Hall concert on 11 May 1962. By a stroke of unforeseeable good fortune the concert marked the triumphant return to Britain of the pianist John Ogdon after his joint victory in the Moscow Tchaikovsky piano competition. There was also the heartening success of the public rehearsals sponsored by Associated Rediffusion and the Society for the Promotion of New Music, at one of which Martin Milner played a violin concerto by David Ellis, later to become B.B.C. Head of Music in Manchester. Another work selected was by Gordon Crosse. Other then unknown composers helped by this scheme were Stephen Dodgson, Christopher Steel, Christopher Headington, Jonathan Harvey, and, most significant of all, John McCabe, who was to become something of a Hallé speciality. Associated Rediffusion also financed the appearances with the Hallé of young soloists. These included the violinist Rodney Friend, the oboist Sarah Francis and the pianists Katrina George and Grace Wilkinson. All fulfilled their early promise. Another example of imaginative patronage which paid off was the assistance given by I.C.I. (Blackley) to the Hallé's principal horn-player, Maurice Handford, in his ambition to become a conductor. He conducted the works' own orchestra and, in May 1960, I.C.I. sponsored a Hallé concert in Manchester at which he conducted Berlioz's *Symphonie Fantastique*. In September 1961 he left the orchestra to concentrate on conducting.

Humour and tragedy jostle each other in an orchestra's history as they do in the music it plays. There was the Hallé player summoned for a parking offence in Huddersfield in May 1961 who told the magistrates: 'I preferred to face the wrath of the police rather than the wrath of Sir John Barbirolli.' He was fined only 7s 6d. A year later the principal piccolo player, William Morris, died in a car accident at the age of fifty-two. He was mourned publicly with Elgar's 'Nimrod'. Probably few players or conductors mourned the Hewitt Street rehearsal room, which was vacated in August 1962 when the orchestra moved into new rehearsal premises in the Zion Institute, Stretford Road. Zion was twice as expensive as Hewitt Street, but the cost was met from increased grants. In November of this year, Manchester City Council gave the Hallé an extra £9,000 in addition to its £9,000 direct grant. New pay awards meant higher prices for Free Trade Hall seats in the 1963-4 season.

The 1963-4 season was Barbirolli's twenty-first with the orchestra. The committee, which now included Philip Godlee's son Richard, decided that he should receive the Hallé's twenty-year-service gold medal. But before the season began in Britain the orchestra in June 1963 undertook an eighteen-day tour of Scandinavia, giving concerts in Norway at the Bergen Festival and in Odda; in Sweden at the Stockholm Festival and in Gothenburg; in Denmark in Copenhagen; and in Finland at the Sibelius Festival in Helsinki. In Bergen the Hallé played Mahler's Fourth and Sibelius's Fifth Symphonies; Sibelius's Second and Fifth Symphonies in Helsinki, to ecstatic praise from the critics; and Nielsen's Fourth Symphony in the Tivoli Gardens, Copenhagen. Some of the players visited Grieg's home and were shown Sibelius's home and grave at Järvenpää by the composer's eldest daughter. There was sadness at the opening concert of the season in Manchester when Barbirolli conducted music in memory of his associate George Weldon, who had died in South Africa in August at the age of fifty-five. An underrated conductor, capable of magnificent performances of such works as the 'Eroica', Walton's First Symphony and Elgar's *In the South*, he had won a big following in Manchester especially at the Summer Proms, which owed much of their success to his friendly, ebullient personality.

Barbirolli's 'gold medal' concert was on 29 September, when he repeated the first programme he had conducted in Manchester in 1943. He presented medals to four players he had engaged that season, Enid Roper (horn), Oliver Bannister (flute, who was about to leave the Hallé for Covent Garden), Tom Cheetham (percussion and librarian) and Donald Shepherd (viola). His own medal was given to him by Martin Milner, who called him a 'Kreisler of conductors' who 'thinks sound'. In the coda of the finale of Tchaikovsky's Fifth Symphony, to quote the *Daily Telegraph's* report of the occasion, 'Sir John put his arms to his sides and conducted this mighty piece by the nodding of his head and no doubt by the expression in his eyes, as we are told his great predecessor Hans Richter used to do. It was as if he was listening to the achievements of two decades.' Barbirolli always enjoyed nostalgia, but he was practical and forward-looking. In April 1964, in Manchester Town Hall, he launched the Trust Fund which the Hallé had set up to mark his anniversary. It had an immediate target of £50,000 to finance special activities, such as concert performances of operas and foreign tours, which could not be financed from grants. He reminded the industrialists and businessmen that in twenty-one years he had trained thirty-two principals who had left for better-paid jobs in the South. 'I always manage to find some more, but it is a little tough to start teaching people all over again because we haven't got the money to keep our fine players.' He added: 'I tell you these things not for my own glory but so that we can achieve higher and higher things in Manchester.' Earlier in the season Clive Smart announced that Weldon would be succeeded by two associate conductors, Lawrence Leonard, forty, and Maurice Handford, thirty-five.

The 1960s were a period of upheaval in music in Britain. With William Glock as B.B.C. Controller of Music, a new spirit of adventure spread through the Promenade Concerts and other B.B.C. enterprises. The Music Programme was instituted (its relic is Radio 3). The music of Schoenberg, Webern and Berg was thoroughly explored; the continental avant-garde of Boulez, Stockhausen, Berio, Ligeti and Nono was welcomed; the British avant-garde of Maxwell Davies, Goehr and Birtwistle (all former students of the Royal Manchester College of Music) was encouraged. Inevitably there was increased criticism of the conservatism of Hallé programmes and of Barbirolli's taste. When this criticism had been voiced a few years earlier, he had replied trenchantly:[1] 'I am a champion of modern music and I am not despondent about it, otherwise I wouldn't conduct the Cheltenham Festival . . . But people pay money to go to concerts after a hard day's work and they are entitled to some consideration. The place for a lot of the experimental works is at the festivals devoted to modern music where finances are put aside solely for that purpose . . . If you look back over my programmes for fourteen years you will find that I have played the largest possible number of modern works consistent with not going bankrupt. One must progress to survive. I don't call Berg's Violin Concerto "experimental". It is an established masterpiece.' A great gulf is fixed between the arbiters of taste among the London critics and intelligentsia and those 'out in the sticks' who have to persuade audiences to attend concerts. In 1963 the Hallé considered omitting Leicester from its schedule. Audiences had fallen away. The local promoter said: 'We have been criticised for not including contemporary music in our programmes, so we included Shostakovich's Symphony No. 5 but with poor response.'

The 1963-4 season resulted in a surplus of £4,339, the first for ten years. Local authority grants had now reached the figure of £90,104. Smart warned the Society that a major problem facing it was the difficulty of obtaining young musicians of the high standard required, a statement it seemed hard to believe when one heard the orchestra of the Royal Manchester College of Music (which Barbirolli regularly conducted) and the college's opera performances. Smart achieved a change in January 1965 which must have pleased his conductor. A few

[1]*The Daily Telegraph*, 4 July 1956.

years earlier, in the programme of the annual Pension Fund concert, Barbirolli had written that it was 'sad and very deplorable' that the Hallé had no proper pension scheme. He cited the example of the Helsinki orchestra, which he had conducted, where the city provided a pension of roughly sixty-five per cent of their salary to players at the age of sixty-three. Smart now dissolved the pension fund, which had relied mainly on charity and gave a maximum pension of £2 a week, and transferred the £50,000 assets to a contributory superannuation and life insurance scheme which the Society had formed several years earlier. Now a player earning £1,000 a year could expect two-thirds of his salary in pension after forty years' service. No more pension fund concerts were given. Another change in January 1965 was the election of Sir Geoffrey Haworth to succeed Duckworth as chairman of the Society. Duckworth's swansong was a renewal of the Hallé's call for a national inquiry into the financing of British symphony orchestras.

In April 1965 Crickmore died of cancer in Ramona, California, at the age of forty-three. The public who knew of their close association in the past may have wondered why Barbirolli paid his former manager no verbal or musical tribute.[1] In December 1964, while recording Elgar's *The Dream of Gerontius* in the Free Trade Hall, Barbirolli had been in severe distress because he had discovered the alarming state of his personal finances. These had been handled in America by Crickmore, who had married Barbirolli's former secretary. This devastating news aged Barbirolli overnight. He had trusted Crickmore implicitly, he had fought for and with him, and now he felt betrayed. Some people who (to their surprise) had been subjected by Crickmore to vitriolic disparagements of Barbirolli, had tried to warn him, but had been brushed aside and regarded as troublemakers. Barbirolli was loyal to a fault to his friends, who were always 'white' for a long time after they deserved a change of shade (conversely with opponents, who were 'black'). This tragic affair overshadowed the next years of Barbirolli's life at a time when his health was deteriorating. He filed a claim in San Diego against Crickmore's estate. Although Mrs Crickmore counter-claimed for damages, alleging that Barbirolli had contributed to her husband's death, the matter was settled out of court in April 1967 when Mrs Crickmore agreed to pay about £35,000 to the Barbirollis from her husband's estate. The Hallé Society had at one time also considered issuing a writ, but did not proceed. Crickmore's

---

[1]The 'official' Hallé tribute to him was the opening concert of the Hallé Summer Proms, which he founded, on 15 June 1965. Lawrence Leonard conducted, and the solo pianist was Julius Katchen, who, ironically, was himself to die at the age of forty-three in 1969.

aim in America had been to try to persuade Barbirolli to break completely with the Hallé and to settle in Houston or some similar centre. To this end he tried to undermine relationships between Barbirolli and Hallé officers such as Duckworth, Yates Lloyd and Smart. He failed, chiefly because Smart was astute.

Ironically, the Hallé's crusade for a national inquiry into orchestras had been Crickmore's creed. It was continued in 1966 when a loss of £404 was reported on the 1964-5 season. During that season the orchestra gave 181 public concerts and undertook forty-three other engagements, still a heavy schedule. The Society was incensed by a report by a committee headed by Lord Goodman that the four London orchestras should receive a basic annual Arts Council grant of £40,000. 'Priority for London' as a criterion was challenged in the Hallé's annual report. This report also referred to Barbirolli's 'never-ending source of inspiration to the Society. Our gratitude is perhaps best expressed by the warmth of the welcome he receives from Manchester audiences on his return from abroad.' Musically this was one of the most rewarding periods of his life. Although plagued by feelings of inadequacy when he went to a foreign orchestra, he nevertheless was revered in Houston, formed happy associations with other American orchestras (particularly Boston, Chicago and 'his' New York), was a welcome guest in Prague, Budapest and Bucharest, and was adored by the Berlin public, where from 1961 he enjoyed an annual 'festival' as the favourite guest conductor of Karajan's Philharmonic. He was, as always, working too hard and his heart mechanism was beginning to falter. For some in Manchester, the Barbirolli magic had worn thin or had never made much appeal as they thought he had stayed too long. But they were in a minority. He was still the Hallé's biggest asset, synonymous with the orchestra. Of course not every concert was the best; but even when things went wrong and his concentration faltered, most of the audience left the hall satisfied and uplifted. 'Never could the words "routine performance" be written for anything performed under his baton' was a typical comment in the non-Mancunian press, and for ninety-five per cent of concerts it was true. He was now a father-figure, a legend. He had his cronies in the orchestra, of course, those who had gone through thick and thin with him, and perhaps some of the younger intake resented this. But he still took an interest in every member of the orchestra and encouraged them to consult him personally about any problems. 'My children of the orchestra' was no empty phrase.

In April 1965 the Hallé went to Switzerland and Italy, playing in Lausanne, Zürich, Berne, Basle and Milan. The same programme, which included Sibelius's Second Symphony, was played in each city but Barbirolli insisted on a three-hour rehearsal each day. He rehearsed Mahler's Sixth Symphony! In November 1966 the Hallé and Barbirolli gave nine concerts in a ten-day tour of Germany, playing in Essen, Leverkusen, Hanover, Hamburg, Kassel, Frankfurt, Nuremberg, Dusseldorf and Viersen. The performance of Brahms's Fourth Symphony in the composer's birthplace, Hamburg, received high praise and a prolonged ovation. The 1965-6 Manchester season was the last in which the midweek concerts were given on Wednesday and Thursday. Henceforward they were to be given on fortnightly Thursdays. The repeat system was now regarded as 'artistically and financially unsound'. Audiences had declined for at least two years. The change was criticised by one member of the Society as 'dictatorial'. Certain other changes also occurred at this time: Maurice Handford was appointed associate conductor (Lawrence Leonard's contract was not renewed) and the Hallé appointed two associate leaders to ease the strain on Martin Milner. They were Sydney Partington and twenty-three-year-old Michael Davis, whose father Eric, a member of the Hallé since 1946, was principal of the second violins. Partington, however, resigned in June 1967. Barbirolli took the Hallé to the Bordeaux Festival in May 1967 to give two concerts. After the 1966-7 season he had relinquished the Houston post of conductor-in-chief and become 'conductor emeritus'. All was now set for the 1967-8 season in Manchester, his twenty-fifth as Hallé conductor. At the opening Sunday concert on 24 September, Laurance Turner was invited back from retirement to share the leader's desk with his successor Martin Milner, and at the first Thursday concert on 28 September Barbirolli presented gifts to the recently retired cellist Sidney Wright, who had first played in the Hallé under Harty in 1921 and had been a permanent member since 1923.

This celebratory season coincided with one of the nation's periodical economic crises. The financial *leitmotiv* of the time was either 'freeze' or 'squeeze'. One manifestation was the fifty per cent reduction in studio broadcasts offered to the Hallé by the B.B.C., a major factor in the Society's loss of £8,590 on the 1966-7 season. The outlook for Barbirolli's jubilee season was equally gloomy, Sir Geoffrey Haworth warned members at the annual meeting in February 1968, unless Manchester City Council increased its direct grant, which had remained at £22,511 a year since 1963 while the Arts Council grant had risen. The treasurer, C. Yates Lloyd, hoped the increase would be in the order of £20,000. The grant from the local authorities' scheme was to be increased by ten per cent over the next five years. 'Manchester is out of proportion with other towns', he commented. In spite of considerable opposition the City Council in September voted an additional £10,000 to the Hallé for the year.

The climax of the Barbirolli jubilee season was the orchestra's longest overseas tour – a six-week visit in June and July 1968 to South America and the West Indies, supported by the British Council and the Hallé Trust Fund. On the eve of departure there was a carnival atmosphere at a 'bon voyage' concert in the Free Trade Hall – on a night of great emotion in Manchester when Manchester United won the European Cup under the management of Matt Busby. Extra time in the match against Benfica robbed Barbirolli of the pleasure of announcing United's victory to the audience (he had a transistor on the side of the platform). During its tour the Hallé travelled 23,000 miles in a specially chartered aircraft to give twenty-three concerts in eight countries: Mexico, Venezuela, Trinidad, Jamaica, Peru, Chile, Argentina and Brazil. In Mexico the concerts were part of the Olympic Games Festival and were given at an altitude of seven thousand feet above sea level, not very good for Barbirolli's heart condition. Denis Matthews and Martin Milner were soloists during the tour and several British works were played, including Britten's *Sinfonia da Requiem*, Elgar's Second Symphony, Rawsthorne's Second Piano Concerto, Walton's Violin Concerto and Vaughan Williams's *The Lark Ascending*. At most concerts, Barbirolli conducted Elgar's *Pomp and Circumstance March No. 1* as an encore to show the flag. Argentine critics were especially lavish with praise. Barbirolli said later, in a radio interview, 'I'd like to remind our listeners in Manchester that we followed the Philadelphia and the Vienna Philharmonic, so we made a huge score against some of the best bowling in the world. And, you know, relations with the Argentine over the Falkland Islands have not been the smoothest, and our ambassador in Buenos Aires told me I did something the Foreign Office had not been able to do. The President came to one of our concerts, and of course the British Ambassador sat in the box with the President in an atmosphere of great cordiality, and he said the image of Britain had changed overnight, through music!' The final concerts were given in Brazil, in Rio de Janeiro, where Martin Milner made the comment: 'It is gratifying to be classed as one of the world's leading orchestras, especially as we are not always awarded this accolade at home.' After the final concert, Sir John entertained the orchestra to dinner.

Before the Manchester concerts in the jubilee season had ended, Barbirolli announced in April that he was to relinquish the title of conductor-in-chief and reduce his engagements with the Hallé. In a letter to Sir Geoffrey Haworth, written from Houston in March, he looked forward to 'many more happy years together'. 'I don't regret one moment of the twenty-five years spent amongst you all,' he wrote. 'It has been my privilege and honour to lead the Hallé to its place amongst the orchestras of the world. To achieve this position I have had to reduce considerably, or renounce altogether, many offers. Now also invitations from the great opera houses to return to my old love – opera – are becoming more and more insistent . . . I must allow a little more time to give myself the pleasure of accepting some of these invitations.' He stressed that he had 'no wish ever to leave our great orchestra' and would be available for tours, broadcasts and recordings. Sir Geoffrey's reply asked Sir John 'to accept the title of Conductor Laureate for Life'.

As earnest of his intentions, Barbirolli took the Hallé in October 1968 to give the closing two concerts of the Montreux Festival, followed by concerts in Geneva, Berne, Basle and Zürich. They then played twice in the Musikvereinssaal, Vienna, and in Salzburg. Finally they gave a concert apiece in Hanover, Hamburg, Hildesheim and Lübeck. On his return to Manchester Barbirolli described the Hallé as 'Manchester's terrific cultural ambassadors abroad,' adding: 'With all due respect to my dear friend Sir Matt Busby, the papers were full of United when they *lost* their match against Estudiantes. But here we are with the equivalent of a 7-0 *win*. I feel that Manchester is not as excited about the Hallé as it should be.' In Vienna, he said, encouraged by rapturous applause 'I stuck my neck out a bit and for the first time ventured to play Viennese waltzes for the encores.' The applause was so prolonged that the orchestra had to be ordered to leave the hall. 'It is awfully good for players to know that in countries where they have their own great orchestras, the Hallé is regarded as among the greats.'

Inevitably Barbirolli's new status led to much speculation on his successor. Gerald Larner, critic of the *Guardian* since 1965 and one of the finest of a distinguished line, wrote that to replace John Barbirolli, you would need another John Barbirolli. Cardus said the new conductor 'need not necessarily be a Harty, a Barbirolli; the crucial thing is that he must *belong*, and not go here and there serving dispassionately Bach, Beethoven, Britten and Mammon'. Another writer, in the *Daily Telegraph*, bemoaned the fall in playing standards during Barbirolli's absences in the 1968-9 season: 'he should be able to return to the city where he is loved and, at specified times each year, conduct an orchestra that at least contains a string section who regularly play both in time and in tune.' Sir Geoffrey Haworth, reporting a £15,000 deficit on the 1967-8 season at the annual meeting in January 1969, assured the Society that the committee would appoint 'the best possible conductor in the least possible time'. The large deficit was mainly the result of a series of national wage awards. It said much for Smart's stewardship of the Society that in July 1969 Manchester City Council more than doubled its direct grant to the Hallé, for one year, from £22,500 to £52,500. Joint talks on future financing were suggested. The usual opposition was voiced, but the extra money was voted eighty-three to thirty-five.

In the 1969 Birthday Honours List, Barbirolli was appointed a Companion of Honour. Other honours and tributes came to him as he neared his seventieth birthday on 2 December. But the increasing seriousness of the heart attacks from which he suffered could no longer be ignored. He began to have what he called 'little blackouts'. One occurred in the Free Trade Hall in October 1969 during the first movement of Mahler's Second Symphony, when it caused him to fail to give one section an important entry. In the following months, disturbing items appeared in newspapers: his collapse in the street in Munich, collapses in Rome and while rehearsing the New Philharmonia in London, a similar event at the King's Lynn Festival. But he always rallied. On 27 March 1970 he gave a dinner party in Manchester for the ten Hallé players who had played over five thousand concerts under his régime. He conducted the last concert of the Hallé Manchester season in May 1970 and took the orchestra to London to play Elgar and Bruckner for the Royal Philharmonic Society. In July he recorded Delius with them and conducted Vaughan Williams and Elgar (the First Symphony) in Ely Cathedral. The last concerts before their annual holiday were, as usual, at the King's Lynn Festival, one of Barbirolli's favourites. He conducted an Elgar programme and, on the last night, Beethoven's Seventh Symphony. Next day the players went on holiday and he went to London to rehearse the New Philharmonia, with whom he was to visit Japan. On 27 July he rehearsed Mahler with the mezzo-soprano Janet Baker, whose artistry and personality he profoundly admired. On 28 July he rehearsed Britten's *Sinfonia da Requiem* and Beethoven's 'Eroica' Symphony. On returning that night to his London flat, he read till after midnight. In the early hours of Wednesday 29 July he had a severe heart attack and was dead on arrival at hospital.

In Manchester that morning the City Council was meeting. When the news came, members stood in silence and prayers were read. His 'adversary' in many a Hallé committee crisis, Sir Leonard Behrens, issued a tribute which was a perfect summing-up: 'he gave himself and in the end he gave his life to the service of the Hallé. His energy was superhuman and his enthusiasm enormous.' Memorial services were held in Westminster Cathedral and in Manchester Cathedral. On 27 September in the Free Trade Hall Maurice Handford, who had paid tribute to his mentor's 'incredible courage', himself bravely conducted Elgar's *The Dream of Gerontius* in Barbirolli's memory. Ronald Dowd and Forbes Robinson were the tenor and baritone soloists. It was a memorable performance, made unforgettable by Janet Baker who, in the Angel's Farewell, falteringly whispered the words while the tears flowed down her cheeks.

Barbirolli had been Hallé conductor for twenty-seven years, ten years shorter than Hallé himself, but he conducted the orchestra in many more concerts. What he achieved – the accomplishment of his 1943 'mission' – has been set forth in the preceding pages. There is no doubt that he sacrificed the financial side of his career to the Hallé. He conducted it for a fraction of the fee he received in Berlin, for example, and he conducted the overseas tours virtually for nothing except expenses. For most of his time in Manchester he had no real contract. 'Let's talk about next season' was enough. Twelve years after his death it is still not possible to exaggerate his influence and magnetism as a musician, his humanity, humour, kindliness and friendliness as a man. He was illustrious, but he was never aloof; thousands of his public met him at some time or other and all took away a warming memory. As an interpreter of music, he was among the élite of conductors. Of each work he performed he had an inner vision of how it appeared to its creator. He took orchestra and listeners into the composer's world. In any orchestra, there are many types – competent, sensitive, brilliant, plodding, eccentric. A conductor must weld them into a corporate identity. Not all will respond alike to his view of a work – sometimes his aim may be too high for them to reach. Barbirolli was conscious that his very positive approach did not appeal to everyone, player or listener, 'they either adore me or I nauseate them'. Most of the Hallé players were British, with concomitant control of deep emotions. Barbirolli, a mixture of English, Latin and Gallic temperaments, would boil up in a flash and as quickly subside. Rehearsals therefore were often tense and nervy – and he required that they should be played to concert standard – but equally often they were radiant and satisfying. Music meant so much to him, took him over so completely, that he found it difficult to realise that it did not mean as much to some others. This led him sometimes to intolerance of what he took to be laziness or indifference. Conversely some players, unable to comprehend a make-up so different from their own, misjudged an extravagant gesture or an exaggerated simile as 'showmanship'. When some of his performances

93

failed to 'come off', it was often because his aim was beyond his players' reach – and few of his players ever knew of the agony of depression he suffered after such occasions because he blamed himself for inadequate realisation of the composer's vision. Generally, his players found his little vanities endearing and they appreciated that even if he was a dictator on the rostrum, he was a benevolent dictator in all his personal dealings with them. A brass player who had left the orchestra some years before told a Hallé player after Barbirolli died – and with tears in his eyes – how much he had missed him, 'but I could have bloody well killed him at times!'

The suggestion that he had a small repertoire and little sympathy with modern music will not survive a glance at his programmes in his time with the Hallé. He had little sympathy with atonal music and none with electronic, but his record as a conductor of twentieth-century works was admirable; and it should be remembered that he often prepared a difficult work for a guest conductor even though it was not a piece he himself was likely to conduct. He once described himself as 'a simple person who is passionately in love with music'. That passion is exemplified by the story of his rehearsing a foreign orchestra in Mahler's First Symphony. In the finale he always required the horn section to stand at the passage where there is written an instruction in the score to that effect. This particular group of horn-players had never met this before and demurred. After some argument, they acquiesced, the principal saying, 'All right Sir John, as it's you we'll do it for you.' Barbirolli slammed the score down on his desk and yelled: 'You're not doing it for me – you're doing it for Mahler'. His faults came from excess of musical sensibilities, never the reverse. ('I don't care if you critics say I overdo things. It's when you say I *underdo* them I'll worry.') The true *sound* of a work – and hence an understanding of its true character – concerned him more than rhythmical precision. In remembering the fervour of his Elgar, the nobility of his Vaughan Williams, the clarity, shape and intensity he brought to Mahler, the splendour of Bruckner and Sibelius under his baton, the virility of his Haydn, the balance of the gruff and the lyrical in Brahms, the lilt and playfulness of his Viennese evenings, the poetry of his Debussy and Ravel, the wayward charm of his Schubert, one remembers above all the grandeur and breadth he brought to music and the lyrical phrasing. A generation of concertgoers find that many works still bring the sight of him to mind: left hand throbbing, his thumb almost an extra baton, or turning to the strings his face alight, or leaning over the cellos, or encouraging the brass and woodwind to give that extra ounce; then when the work was over, talking to the players, sharing his enthusiasm with them. One can even hear in certain passages that counterpoint of groans wrung from him by his exertions.

Sir Geoffrey Haworth was perceptive when, in his memorial address in Manchester Cathedral, he said that Barbirolli had needed 'the rock of Manchester' on which to build his worldwide career. Undoubtedly there was an element of love-hate in his relationship with the Hallé. He thought the city fathers were mean, he cursed the Hallé committee up hill and down dale, he knew that compared with the Berlin Philharmonic his players were not of international class. Yet, however often he threatened to leave, he never meant it. Too much of his life was involved with the Hallé, too many memories, too much triumph, too much heartbreak, too much loyalty, for him to sever the tie. Creating and educating new audiences in the North satisfied him. He thrived on the challenge of municipal skinflints, however much they annoyed him. He enjoyed showing London what the provinces could do. What he achieved with the Hallé was a glorious triumph against the odds. But what he might and could have achieved if the city had really shown a true appreciation of his worth could be heard by anyone who attended one of his concerts with the Berlin Philharmonic.

XIII—*The music, 1958-70*

On the evening of 26 August 1958, the day Vaughan Williams died, the Hallé played at the London Proms. Barbirolli conducted the *Tallis Fantasia* in memory of his friend and he opened the midweek series in Manchester with the same work, followed by the composer's Ninth and last Symphony. In this 1958-9 season, Barbirolli also conducted Mahler's Second Symphony, Nielsen's Fourth Symphony, Strauss's *Don Quixote*, Walton's *Partita*, Holst's *The Planets* and Moeran's Violin Concerto in which Laurance Turner, the retired leader, returned as soloist.

With Barbirolli away in the United States for several weeks, there were more guest conductors than usual. Three made their débuts with the Hallé: Rudolf Kempe (3 December 1958, a night of thick fog) in Martinu's *Frescoes of Piero della Francesca*, Strauss's *Don Juan* and Brahms's Fourth Symphony; Constantin Silvestri (11 February 1959) in Prokofiev and Tchaikovsky; and Colin Davis (7 December 1958), who introduced Stravinsky's *The Fairy's Kiss* to the concerts. (Just as there are some great batsmen who never score many runs at Old Trafford – Bradman, for example – so some conductors never really 'hit it off' in Manchester. Sir Colin is among these.) George Weldon introduced Shostakovich's Eleventh Symphony and John Joubert's Piano Concerto, Charles Groves (with Heather Harper as soprano soloist) on 23 November marked the centenary of the Hallé Choir by conducting Haydn's *The Creation*, which Hallé had chosen for the choir's first performance on 3 April 1858, and there were visits by Boult, Sargent, Vilem Tausky, Jascha Horenstein, Tzipine, and Howard Mitchell. A visit by the B.B.C. Symphony Orchestra under Rudolf Schwarz brought the first Manchester performance of Tippett's Piano Concerto, soloist Ilona Kabos. Soloists in the season included Paul Badura-Skoda, Hans Richter-Haaser, Curzon, Geza Anda, Abbey Simon and Gyorgy Cziffra (pianists); Ion Voicu and Berl Senofsky (violinists) and Milos Sadlo (cellist). The visiting Royal Philharmonic's concert under Herman Lindars included Strauss's *Symphonia Domestica*, by-passed by the Hallé since 1906.

Besides such of his favourites as Sibelius's Second Symphony and Debussy's *La Mer*, Barbirolli conducted Bartók's *Concerto for Orchestra* (on his sixtieth birthday), Beethoven's Ninth Symphony and Mahler's Ninth Symphony and *Lieder eines fahrenden Gesellen* (Kerstin Meyer) in the 1959-60 season. Claudio Arrau and Artur Rubinstein appeared with him as soloists in, respectively, Beethoven's C minor and Brahms's B flat Piano Concertos. George Weldon's programmes included Humphrey Searle's Second Piano Concerto (Clive Lythgoe), Vaughan Williams's *Job*, Kurt Atterberg's Sixth Symphony, Medtner's First Piano Concerto, Blacher's *Paganini Variations* and a performance of Rachmaninov's Second Symphony which W. R. Sinclair of the *Daily Telegraph* (who attended nearly every Hallé concert from 1921 until his death in 1980, for thirty-six years as a critic) complained was cut in a 'cavalier' manner. Guest conductors included Kempe, Henryk Czyz, Tzipine, Pierino Gamba, Boult (Beethoven's Mass in D), Lindars (*Rite of Spring*, this time with the Hallé itself), Silvestri and George Hurst. A highlight was the visit of the Royal Philharmonic with Beecham on 27 November, which caused John Robert-Blunn of the *Manchester Evening News* to write: 'To judge by the reception . . . anyone would think that Manchester was cut off in the wilds and the Hallé Orchestra and Sir John Barbirolli had never been heard of . . . The performance of Mozart's 39th Symphony made one feel that the gods had come down among us.' During this season Barbirolli unearthed the vocal version of Tchaikovsky's *Romeo and Juliet*. When he conducted it in London, Martin Cooper described it as a 'curiosity' and added: 'The text is also singularly unfortunate and Victoria Elliott and Charles Craig found themselves engaged in what appeared to be a passionate discussion between two bird-watchers disputing the identity of what seemed a nightingale to one and a lark to the other. When each changed his opinion for that of the other, the audience was visibly amused. The singers showed hardly more conviction in their singing than in their opinions on ornithology.' The London critics were none too laudatory in their opinions of the Hallé at this time. Donald Mitchell, reviewing a Schubert concert in the Festival Hall in July 1960 described Barbirolli's interpretations as 'gripping in detail, but rarely revealing the mastery of a complete design . . . The strings produced far too little fine tone and . . . insufficient attention was paid by any section to differentiations of the lower range of dynamics.' Michael Winfield, principal oboe since 1953, left the orchestra at the end of this season, and Joyce Aldous, the timpanist, retired. She was succeeded by Jack Gledhill.

In 1960-1 important works by Schoenberg and Webern appeared in the programmes for the first time. The former's *Five Orchestral Pieces* was conducted by Sir Eugene Goossens on 19 April and the latter's *Six Pieces for Orchestra*, op. 6, by George Weldon on 8 February. Fricker's Viola Concerto, played by Herbert Downes, was in a Boult programme; Berthold Lehmann, conductor at Hallé's birthplace Hagen, introduced Rolf Liebermann's *Furioso*; a Finnish newcomer Tauno Hannikainen conducted Sibelius's Fourth Symphony; Weldon conducted Francis Burt's *Espressione Orchestrale*, Vaughan Williams's *Sea Symphony*, Barber's Symphony, and a programme of three Mozart piano concertos (Nos. 9, 17 and 24) with Denis Matthews; Lindars introduced Khatchaturyan's Second Symphony; and George Hurst conducted a Schumann 150th anniversary programme, including the concertos for piano and cello, and an extra concert at Belle Vue on 2 March when David Oistrakh played Brahms's Violin Concerto, Igor Oistrakh Beethoven's, and father and son joined forces in Bach's D minor. Other guest conductors were Herbert Menges, Tzipine and Bernard Herrmann. The Hungarian State Symphony Orchestra, under Janós Ferencsik, played Bartók, Kodály and Beethoven on 10 November. A guest conductor at Sheffield in December, in his own edition of *Messiah*, was Walter Goehr, who sadly collapsed and died after the performance. Among the season's soloists were Isaac Stern (Sibelius Violin Concerto) and Henryk Szeryng, and the pianists Gina Bachauer, Daniel Wayenberg, Peter Katin, Julius Katchen, and Moiseiwitsch. Barbirolli's programmes included the two-piano concerto by Dussek (last played in Manchester by Hallé and Hecht on 5 February 1863), Kodály's *Peacock Variations*, Ravel's *Shéhérazade* (soprano, Irma Kolassi), Britten's *Nocturne* (tenor soloist, Gerald

English) and an astonishing Mahler centenary programme on 19 October with the combined Hallé and B.B.C. Northern Orchestras which comprised his Seventh Symphony and Nielsen's Fifth Symphony. Donald Mitchell, in the *Daily Telegraph*, described how the Mahler 'held a huge audience enthralled . . . Sir John's grasp of the work rarely faltered . . . It was a performance full of passionate insights.' Yet the big event for Barbirolli was his first Bach *St Matthew Passion* on 26 March 1961, performed complete and sung in German. The soloists were Alexander Young (Evangelist), Elsie Morison, Kerstin Meyer, Max Worthley, Trevor Anthony and Nowakowski (Christus) with the Hallé Choir in superb form and Dennis Nesbitt (viola da gamba) and Valda Aveling (harpsichord). 'When a great conductor, at the age of sixty-one, spends five years of work and study on one of the noblest products of the human mind,' the *Telegraph* critic wrote, 'preparing every note and part, it is clear that theoretically the result should be a major artistic experience. In practice, the high expectations were fulfilled.' Ernest Bradbury, of the *Yorkshire Post*, described the result as 'a kind of restored and cleaned masterpiece, to which nothing has been added but in which every detail now appears fresh and – in a new sense – vital.' Because he is usually associated with the Romantic repertoire, less than proper attention has been paid to Barbirolli's interest in baroque music. His own arrangements of Handel, Corelli, Purcell, Pergolesi and others are very stylish in the best sense. In his version of *Messiah*, while not attempting the full-scale return to 'authenticity' of Christopher Hogwood and others, he devoted considerable time and trouble to restoring as much of Handel's original conception as was compatible with the requirements of balance using a large choir – and this in 1951. In the Bach *Passion*, his principal achievement was a reconciliation of scholarship with commonsense musicianship. Also he instantly incorporated H. C. Robbins Landon's corrections into Haydn symphonies.

Barbirolli repeated the *Passion* in the 1961-2 season on 15 April. Other major works he conducted were the Adagio from Mahler's Tenth Symphony, Berg's Concerto for piano, violin and thirteen wind instruments ('this one might hurt a bit,' he warned the audience beforehand, like a kindly dentist), Bruckner's Ninth Symphony (with the combined Hallé and B.B.C. Northern), Shostakovich's First Cello Concerto (Milos Sadlo), Prokofiev's Fifth Piano Concerto, Delius's *Appalachia*, Debussy's *Nocturnes*, Ravel's complete *Daphnis and Chloë* ballet and Verdi's *Requiem*. Weldon conducted Malcolm Arnold's Fifth Symphony, and to mark German's centenary, a concert performance of *Merrie England*; Hannikainen returned to conduct Sibelius's Sixth

Symphony; Carlo Felice Cillario brought Malipiero's Sixth Symphony; and Lawrence Leonard marked Walton's sixtieth birthday with the Second Symphony. Other guest conductors were Oscar Danon, Massimo Freccia, and Herman Lindars. Rudolf Kempe came with the Bamberg Symphony Orchestra on 18 October, with Egk's *Caribbean Variations* as the novelty. The season's soloists included the pianists Gary Graffman and David Wilde (in Poulenc's *Aubade* for piano and eighteen instruments) and Archie Camden, who played Mozart's Bassoon Concerto with Barbirolli.

The Manchester season in 1962-3 opened at Belle Vue on 16 September when David Oistrakh and Barbirolli collaborated in a wonderful performance of Beethoven's Violin Concerto. The Free Trade Hall season opened with Brahms's B flat Piano Concerto played by one of Barbirolli's favourite soloists, Gina Bachauer. Among the works Barbirolli conducted were Shostakovich's Fifth and Nielsen's Fourth Symphonies, the first English performance of Saeverud's Violin Concerto (André Gertler), the *St Matthew Passion*, Mahler's Fourth Symphony, Bruckner's Eighth Symphony (combined Hallé and B.B.C. Northern Orchestras in 'beautifully flexible and fine-shaded playing'), Liszt's *Faust Symphony*, with the choral ending, Vaughan Williams's Fifth and Sixth Symphonies and Elgar's Violin Concerto with Martin Milner giving a performance, according to the *Daily Telegraph*, 'in which technique, poetry and the grand manner were inextricably fused'. Weldon, in what was to be his last season, introduced Kodály's Symphony. Other first Hallé performances were of Orff's *Carmina Burana* (Handford, 11 November), Searle's Second Symphony (Leonard), Martinu's Fifth Symphony (Karel Ancerl), Hindemith's Symphony in E flat (Hurst), and Vogel's *Six Fragments from Thyl Claes*, conducted by Cillario and with Dorothy Dorow as soprano. Alvar Lidell spoke the narration in the Vogel 'with all the clarity, and considerably more than the dramatic emphasis, of the six o'clock news', as a critic wrote who found the work 'Teutonic bombast'. Stravinsky's eightieth birthday was marked by Lindars on 17 October with the Symphony in C and *Movements* (solo pianist Charles Rosen). Other guest conductors were Walter Hendl, of Chicago, Mladen Jagust, Hannikainen (Rachmaninov's Second Symphony) and, making his Hallé début, Bernard Haitink, who conducted Haydn, Prokofiev and Brahms on 31 October 1962. Boult conducted *Messiah* at Belle Vue on 9 December, notable for the first Hallé appearance of the contralto Janet Baker. Compared with the 'aching poignancy' of Ferrier, wrote W. R. Sinclair in the *Telegraph*, she sounded 'mildly elegiac'. (Within a short time, however, she was to cast as powerful a spell as Ferrier.) The soprano was Elizabeth Harwood and the tenor and bass were Richard Lewis and Donald Bell. Among the solo pianists at the concerts were Valda Aveling, Badura-Skoda, Liv Glaser, John Ogdon and, for the first time, Daniel Barenboim (Mozart's 27th concerto with Barbirolli on 13 January 1963). The violinists included Szeryng and Rodney Friend. The season remains fresh in some minds, though, for the appearance as guest conductor on 27 February of Nadia Boulanger, then aged seventy-five, and the first woman to conduct a complete Hallé concert (Ethel Smyth conducted one of her own overtures in 1915). Her programme comprised her sister Lili's Psalm 24 (tenor soloist Ryland Davies), Mozart's E flat Piano Concerto (No. 22, K. 482, soloist Idil Biret), Hindemith's *Concert Music* and Fauré's *Requiem* (Eileen Poulter and John Shirley-Quirk). In the *Requiem*, Boulanger evoked its serenity and radiance without sentimentality but with tenderness and the most graceful phrasing.

Barbirolli's twenty-first season, 1963-4, began with a visit on 25 September by the Moscow Philharmonic, conducted by Kyril Kondrashin, who gave the first Manchester performance of Shostakovich's Eighth Symphony. Igor and David Oistrakh were soloists in Mozart's Sinfonia Concertante, David playing the viola. Barbirolli indulged his own preferences and conducted many of his favourite works: Elgar's and Sibelius's Second Symphonies, Vaughan Williams's *Tallis Fantasia* and Eighth Symphony, Mozart's last three symphonies, *Messiah*, Bruckner's Seventh Symphony (of the London performance, Peter Stadlen wrote in the *Daily Telegraph* that it 'persuaded one that this music belongs to the greatest we have'), Elgar's *Falstaff* and *The Dream of Gerontius*, Chausson's *Poème de l'amour et de la mer* (Kerstin Meyer), Nielsen's Fourth Symphony, Brahms's B flat Piano Concerto with Rubinstein, Mozart's A major (K. 488) Piano Concerto with Curzon, Strauss's Oboe Concerto with Lady Barbirolli as soloist, a Wagner evening, and Mahler's Second Symphony with Erna Spoorenberg and Janet Baker as the solo singers. But the rest of the season was also distinguished. It included the first Manchester performance, on 10 November 1963, of Britten's *War Requiem*, conducted by Meredith Davies, with Heather Harper, Peter Pears and John Shirley-Quirk as the solo singers. Pierre Monteux, at eighty-eight, conducted an enriching Brahms First Symphony. Haitink conducted Stravinsky's *Rite of Spring*, Tzipine Prokofiev's Seventh Symphony; Antal Dorati Walton's recent *Variations on a Theme of Hindemith* and Hindemith's *Weber Metamorphosis*; Boult Vaughan Williams's *Pastoral Symphony*; and Carlo Zecchi some Pizzetti and Schumann's Third

Symphony. Maurice Handford conducted Shostakovich's Twelfth Symphony (18 March) and a Strauss centenary concert which revived *Also sprach Zarathustra* for Manchester after fifty-eight years. Lawrence Leonard conducted Berlioz's *Romeo and Juliet* complete, the singers being Josephine Veasey, Alexander Young and Heinz Rehfuss (19 February). Among the soloists in the season were the new favourites such as Ogdon, Barenboim (with the English Chamber Orchestra under John Pritchard) and Gary Graffman, and some new names – Ingrid Haebler and Peter Frankl among pianists, Salvatore Accardo among violinists. Another visiting orchestra was the Bavarian Radio Symphony, under Kubelik, on 7 May. Its programme included Janáček's *Taras Bulba*. The season in Manchester ended with a 'celebration' concert attended by the Society's patron, the Princess Royal, and civic heads from all parts of the North-West.

Near the beginning of the 1964-5 season coming events cast their shadow before them when James Loughran conducted the Hallé for the first time, on 11 October, in Rossini's *William Tell* overture, the Handel–Harty *Water Music*, three dances from Falla's *Tricorne* and Rimsky-Korsakov's *Scheherazade*. He had conducted in Manchester the previous June during the Royal Opera's visit. Another important newcomer to the Hallé rostrum, on 7 February 1965, was the fifty-year-old Latvian conductor Arvid Yansons, joint chief conductor with Mravinsky of the Leningrad Philharmonic since 1952. He conducted two programmes of Russian music, including Prokofiev's Fifth Symphony and *Romeo and Juliet* suite, and provoked W. R. Sinclair of the *Daily Telegraph* to write: 'There was no doubting Mr Yansons's authority and inspiring influence, and he in turn found the Hallé players at their most responsive and eloquent.' The Prokofiev symphony 'might have been an established item in the Hallé's repertory, such were the precision and accuracy'. Three Shostakovich works were performed this season, none of them in a Yansons concert. Barbirolli revived the First Symphony and Handford the Fifth. Handford put what was then still the composer's only Violin Concerto into a Summer Prom in June 1965, with Manoug Parikian as soloist. Other Handford occasions were Hindemith's *Mathis der Maler* symphony (at a concert in tribute to the artist L. S. Lowry, who would much have preferred Bellini), Brahms's Double Concerto with Yan Pascal and his father Paul Tortelier as soloists (Tortelier, incidentally, had just conducted the Hallé at three concerts in North Wales), and the belated first Hallé performance of Tippett's *A Child of our Time* on 28 February, with Jennifer Vyvyan, Alfreda Hodgson, William McAlpine and Forbes Robinson the solo quartet with the Hallé Choir. Lawrence

Leonard conducted Arnold's Fourth and Searle's Fifth Symphonies. The name of Messiaen was imported into the Hallé repertoire by Tzipine, who conducted *L'Ascension* on 11 November 1964. David Willcocks conducted Britten's *War Requiem*, Boult Vaughan Williams's *London* and Schubert's Ninth Symphonies, and there were visits from Walter Süsskind (Suk's *Fairy Tale*), Francesco Mander, Alexander Gibson and Colin Davis, with whom Yehudi Menuhin returned to the Hallé platform in Beethoven's concerto. The B.B.C. Symphony Orchestra, under Antal Dorati, gave different programmes at its concerts on 7 and 8 April, introducing to Manchester the pianist Stephen Bishop who played the Fourth and Fifth Concertos by Beethoven.

Barbirolli's programmes included both Elgar symphonies, No. 1 on his sixty-fifth birthday and No. 2 in Manchester Cathedral, Bruckner's Third Symphony, a Wagner evening of *Ring* extracts (when I described him as 'a Mime of the rostrum, forging swords of sound'), Mahler *Wunderhorn* songs enchantingly sung by Irmgard Seefried, Rawsthorne's Second Piano Concerto (George Hadjinikos), Mozart piano concertos with Curzon and Barenboim, Verdi's *Requiem* and Mahler's Sixth Symphony. The last-named he and the Hallé had first performed in Leeds in January 1965. The Manchester performance was on 5 May, and they took it to the London Proms on 26 July, made the occasion for the presentation of the Mahler Medal to Barbirolli by its previous English recipient Deryck Cooke. The Prom performance, said Colin Mason, now a London critic of the *Daily Telegraph*, had 'a frenzied reception'. He described it as declaring the conductor's 'devotion for and close study of Mahler in every bar. It is a devotion that he has shown in Mahler performances over many years.'

The year 1965 also marked the centenary of the Hallé's association with Bradford, where Frederick Delius's father had been among those in the 1860s who invited Mr Hallé to take his band to Yorkshire. One of the principal centenary events was the first performance of the Second Symphony by the former Hallé trumpeter, Arthur Butterworth, conducted by Boult on 31 October. It was also the centenary of Nielsen's birth, which gave Barbirolli an excuse to include the Fourth Symphony in a July Buxton Festival concert, thus also answering critics of the conservative nature of the Hallé programmes at this festival since Crickmore had founded it in 1959. From Buxton, Barbirolli took the Hallé back to the Cheltenham Festival on its twentieth anniversary, their first visit since 1959. They played Fricker's First Symphony, of which they had given the first performance at the 1950 festival, to a packed hall. 'They are still the biggest draw at the box office that the festival has known,' Mason wrote, 'and many will hope that a programme formula can be found that will bring them back annually.' One other event of the 1964-5 season must be recorded here. At a Festival Hall concert by the Hallé and Sir John on 7 April 1965, the nineteen-year-old soloist in Elgar's Cello Concerto was Jacqueline du Pré. In the *Daily Telegraph*, Martin Cooper remarked that it was 'an extraordinary thing that so young a player should have identified herself so completely . . . with this nostalgic, autumnal work of an ageing composer'.

Colin Mason had left the *Manchester Guardian* in 1964 but he had left Manchester in 1960, having been succeeded by his deputy J. H. Elliot, a critic of much sensibility and perception whose wariness of extremes of opinion extended as much to his enthusiasms as to his dislikes, both of music and its performance. From 1962, Elliot was assisted by the twenty-six-year-old Gerald Larner, who took over as senior critic in 1965. He had no such wariness and soon replaced Mason in the minds of some of the public as the supposed 'scourge' of the Hallé – an undeserved notoriety for, as much as Johnstone and Cardus, he was insistent that 'only the best' was good enough for the Hallé and his jealous guarding of high standards was, from a different viewpoint, as dedicated as Barbirolli's. The *Guardian* critic no longer enjoyed the almost exclusive domination that had been the lot of Newman, Langford and Cardus. Since 1945 the *Daily Telegraph* had employed two, sometimes three, music critics in Manchester and from 1960 the lively, inquiring and sometimes irreverent pen of John Robert-Blunn had added weight to the columns of the *Manchester Evening News.* In any case the *Guardian*'s interest in Manchester was on the wane. The city's name had been removed from its title in 1959 and later it was to transfer almost the whole of its publishing operation to London, the editor having moved from Cross Street to Fleet Street (actually Gray's Inn Road) in 1963. Indeed, its continued coverage of Hallé concerts may be seen as the last vestige of a conscience about the city of its birth and greatness.

Music's most important 1965 centenary fell within the 1965-6 season, the hundredth anniversary of Sibelius's birth. The Hallé for the third time performed the seven symphonies in a season, but this time not in chronological order and not all conducted by Barbirolli. The centenary was on 8 December and that evening Barbirolli conducted the Fifth and Seventh Symphonies and the Violin Concerto (Martin Milner). During the season Barbirolli conducted the First Symphony, Handford the Second, Leonard the Third, Hannikainen the Fourth and Jussi Jalas (Sibelius's son-in-law) the Sixth. Hannikainen also

103

introduced a contemporary Finnish work, Kokkonen's *Opus Sonorum*. Two other composers new to the programmes were Richard Rodney Bennett, whose *Aubade* for piano was played by Julius Katchen, with Leonard conducting, on 30 March, and Dallapiccola, represented by three extracts from the ballet *Marsia*, conducted by Massimo Freccia on 20 March. Two Shostakovich symphonies were performed, No. 9 under Yansons (who also conducted Berlioz's *Symphonie Fantastique*) and No. 10 under Leonard. Boult, besides Vaughan Williams's Fourth Symphony, introduced Malcolm Williamson's Third Piano Concerto (with the composer as soloist) and Leonard conducted his *Sinfonietta*. Stravinsky's *Symphony in Three Movements* was conducted by Haitink and his opera-oratorio *Oedipus Rex* by Handford on 3 April 1966. Gerald English sang Oedipus and Johanna Peters Jocasta. W. R. Sinclair called the performance 'a triumph of perceptive, almost intuitive conducting . . . and the pity was that so few were present'. Handford also conducted Bax's Fourth Symphony (neglected since 1937), Kodály's *Concerto for Orchestra*, Orff's *Carmina Burana*, Liebermann's *Furioso*, and the first performance of John McCabe's *Variations on a Theme by Hartmann* (24 November 1965), hailed by a *Telegraph* critic as 'a dazzling display of orchestral virtuosity which never becomes eccentric or wilfully perverse'. Handford was also the conductor for Ida Haendel's performance of Dvořák's Violin Concerto, its first at the Hallé since 1941, and for the Manchester début of the pianist John Lill in Mozart's B flat concerto (No. 27, K. 595) on 17 November 1965. Another joint Hallé début, on 7 November, was that of the conductor Claudio Abbado – also his English début – in a suite from Prokofiev's *Chout* and Dvořák's Eighth Symphony, and of the pianist Martha Argerich in Chopin's E minor concerto. There was also the Manchester début on 10 October of Mstislav Rostropovich in Dvořák's Cello Concerto with the Moscow Philharmonic under Kondrashin. Another major event was the performance on 13 February by the combined Hallé and B.B.C. Northern Orchestras under George Hurst of Schoenberg's vast *Gurrelieder*, with a fine team of soloists in Sylvia Fisher, Janet Baker, John Lanigan, Kenneth Neate and Forbes Robinson, with the Hallé Choir, B.B.C. Northern Singers and Nelson Arion Male Voice Choir and Alvar Lidell as narrator.

Barbirolli's 1965-6 programmes included Britten's *Sinfonia da Requiem*, Kaminski's *Israeli Sketches*, Nielsen's Fifth Symphony preceded by Ogdon playing Brahms's B flat Piano Concerto, Bruckner's Ninth Symphony ('a great and surely unforgettable interpretation' said Gerald Larner), preceded by Barenboim playing Beethoven's G major concerto, Haydn's C major Cello Concerto with

Jacqueline du Pré (13 October), Beethoven's Ninth Symphony, Debussy's *Nocturnes*, Satie's *Two Gymnopédies*, and Bartók's Second Piano Concerto (Geza Anda) and *Divertimento*. He conducted another Wagner evening (Sylvia Fisher deputising at the last minute for the Finnish soprano Anita Välkki, who had sung in the previous two seasons), and a complete concert performance of Puccini's *Madama Butterfly* on 11 May with Elizabeth Vaughan as Butterfly and David Hughes as Pinkerton. There was much talk at this time about building an opera house in Manchester. In the programme for *Butterfly*, Sir John wrote that he would welcome this 'if it were really done on a proper scale, with a pit to hold an opera orchestra with a complete string section. This is essential – if Manchester's going to spend this money, it must spend it properly and make sure it can really put on grand opera, not baby grand.' A *Telegraph* critic described the performance as 'a revelation of the dramatic genius' of the score and Barbirolli's conducting as 'an intuitive feeling for the ebb and flow of the music'. But he said there were moments when one wished that Hallé conductors 'could have a really full international-status body of strings at their disposal'. A London colleague a few days earlier had wished (for Nielsen's Fifth Symphony) that 'the Hallé strings had more strength and a more pronounced bloom to their upper tone'. A rather special, if not unique, occasion was connected with the first Manchester performances on 13 and 14 April of Mahler's Fifth Symphony. The performance on the 14th (and on the 17th in London) was a tribute to Neville Cardus to celebrate his fifty-year association with the *Guardian*. Presenting the seventy-seven-year-old critic with a photostat copy of the score of the Mahler symphony containing the marks he (Barbirolli) had made in preparing the performance, Sir John saluted Cardus as 'a critic who loves music'. Cardus, recalling Richter and Harty, told the audience that 'some peculiar destiny has watched over the Hallé. When your hall was destroyed and your orchestra finished, destiny gave you the one man you needed. He stands first among the conductors whom I call interpreters and artists, a poetic conductor.' Barbirolli again took the Hallé to Cheltenham, where on 9 July he conducted McCabe's First Symphony, repeating it in London later the same week, and to the Edinburgh Festival (with Berg's Violin Concerto) in September. From August 1966 the Hallé Choir had a new chorus master, John Rust replacing Eric Chadwick, who had succeeded Bardgett in 1956 after being the choir's accompanist since 1950.

As a preliminary to the 1966-7 season Barbirolli conducted a concert on 4 September in the Free Trade Hall at which the Jewish National Fund marked the naming after Sir John of an estate in Netua, Israel,

105

to commemorate his work with the Israel Philharmonic Orchestra. Vladimir Ashkenazy was soloist in Beethoven's First Piano Concerto. The season surveyed the bulk of Elgar's major output with Barbirolli conducting the symphonies, Cello Concerto (du Pré), *Sea Pictures* (Janet Baker), and *Gerontius*, with the soloists of the Hallé's 1964 recording, Janet Baker, Richard Lewis and Kim Borg. When this team also performed the work in London, Colin Mason found Janet Baker 'superlative' but that Barbirolli 'applied a perpetual *espressivissimo* that weighed the music down heavily'. Handford conducted *The Kingdom* on 2 April, with Sheila Armstrong, Pamela Bowden, William McAlpine and Peter Walker, its first Hallé performance since 1927 and miserably attended (and he also conducted a Northern School of Music performance of *The Apostles* on 23 February); Boult conducted the Violin Concerto (Bronislav Gimpel). It was an arduous season for Handford who, besides conducting most of the Industrial Concerts and the Summer Proms, conducted Tippett's *Concerto for Orchestra* on 5 October ('the foyers in the interval afterwards were fairly abuzz with conversation, not all of it about the weather', a *Telegraph* critic wrote), Vaughan Williams's Fifth Symphony and *Partita*, Ginastera's *Concertante Variations*, Britten's *Serenade*, with Gerald English (tenor) and Julian Baker, the Hallé's principal horn, Berlioz's *Requiem* (12 February 1967, its first Hallé performance since Harty's in 1930), the British première (in Sheffield on 29 October) of Wilfred Josephs's *Requiem*, and the first Hallé performance on 16 October of Stravinsky's beautiful *Apollo*. Arvid Yansons conducted two Shostakovich works, the Fifth Symphony and the Second Piano Concerto (Dmitri Paperno); Norman Del Mar revived Strauss's *Le bourgeois gentilhomme* suite; Charles Groves brought the R.L.P.O. in Walton's First Symphony; Karel Ancerl conducted Stravinsky's *Petrushka*; the Jugoslav Zivojin Zdravkovich conducted Bartók's Third Piano Concerto (Hadjinikos); Abbado had Martha Argerich again as soloist in Prokofiev's Third Piano Concerto; and other conductors were Tzipine and Freccia. Barbirolli's soloists included Gina Bachauer and Geza Anda and the big works he conducted included Bartók's *Concerto for Orchestra*, Berg's Violin Concerto (Szeryng), Bach's concerto for violin, oboe and continuo (Szeryng, Evelyn Rothwell and Valda Aveling), Bruckner's Seventh Symphony, preceded by Barenboim playing Mozart's D minor concerto (No. 20, K. 466), Janáček's *Taras Bulba*, McCabe's First Symphony, Menotti's Violin Concerto (Fredell Lack) and, as the climax to the season, Mahler's Third Symphony, its first Manchester performances on 10 and 11 May, with Helen Watts as contralto soloist. Gerald Larner wrote in the *Guardian* that the Hallé had done nothing so memorable as this 'monumental interpretation'. He had never heard a live or recorded performance that characterised the first movement so vividly – 'such orchestral robustness, freshness, uninhibited tunefulness and bare-faced cockiness is not often heard'. In the final Adagio, 'Sir John's treatment was not rapt and prayer-like, but extraordinarily firm and clear in outline'.

After its by now customary visit to the London Proms, during which the Russian pianist Victoria Postnikova was the soloist with Barbirolli in Tchaikovsky's First Concerto, the Hallé's Manchester season for 1967-8 opened with Strauss's *Ein Heldenleben*. Although this was Barbirolli's 'silver jubilee' season, the programmes were no mere wallow in nostalgia. Twenty-two works were performed for the first time at these concerts. Besides the main Thursday and Sunday series, there were eight 'special' concerts, four choral evenings and eight extra concerts of various kinds. Altogether there were fifty Manchester concerts excluding the Industrials and Proms, the most for many years. Barbirolli conducted Bartók's Sonata for two pianos and percussion, Poulenc's Concerto for two pianos, Debussy's *Images*, Rawsthorne's Second Piano Concerto (Hadjinikos), Berlioz's *Harold in Italy* (with Sydney Errington, the Hallé's superb principal viola), Nielsen's Fourth, Bruckner's Eighth and Elgar's First Symphonies, Schoenberg's *Pelleas and Melisande*, Beethoven's Choral Symphony (with a new English translation by Basil Swift), Bliss's Piano Concerto (Ogdon), Britten's Violin Concerto (Wanda Wilkomirska), Vaughan Williams's Fifth and *London* Symphonies, Mahler's First Symphony, Walton's Violin Concerto (Milner), Bach's *St Matthew Passion* (soloists Alexander Young, Robert Tear, John Shirley-Quirk, Kim Borg, Sheila Armstrong and Janet Baker), Mahler's *Das Lied von der Erde* (Janet Baker and Ronald Dowd) and Verdi's *Requiem* (Gwyneth Jones, Janet Baker, David Hughes, replacing Pavarotti, and Kim Borg). Of Janet Baker's singing in the Mahler, a *Daily Telegraph* critic wrote: 'We again have an artist at whose every note we clutch as if we would hoard beauty like Alberich's gold.'

All the foregoing was in addition to Barbirolli's favourite symphonies of Brahms, Beethoven and Sibelius, and dozens of smaller works. Barenboim played Beethoven's C minor concerto with him, Seefried sang Mahler, Evelyn Rothwell played Bax, Schneiderhan played Bruch and Ruth Fermoy the Schumann. In Liszt's A major concerto the pianist was Clifford Curzon and Larner wrote next day: 'A thesis could be written on exactly when and why Sir John adopts the audio-visual aid of tapping on his desk at the orchestra. Usually it suggests that a performance has not been well prepared and the normally accepted silent stick technique is not sufficient to keep the orchestra together. Intolerably much of it was heard during . . . Liszt's concerto in which the orchestral playing was coarse, vulgar, ill-disciplined and a blustering shame . . . A world apart in accomplishment as well as in sympathy with the music's personality was the interpretation of Nielsen's Fourth Symphony.' If this was the worst and best of Barbirolli and the Hallé, there was plenty of the best. A 'most memorable' performance in London of Elgar's Second Symphony led Gerald Abraham to write of 'an enduring monument to all the nobility, the splendour of thought, the idealism that are despised and rejected and mocked in England today and that seem to be deserting her for ever'. The season's climax came on 16 and 18 May with magnificent concert performances of Verdi's *Otello*, with Pier Miranda Ferraro in the title-role, Elizabeth Vaughan as Desdemona and John Shaw as Iago, a revelation of all that Barbirolli might have achieved in the opera house if he had not devoted twenty-five years of his life to the Hallé in Manchester, Bradford, Sheffield and the rest.

Several other highlights of a remarkable season were to the credit of Maurice Handford: Messiaen's *Turangalila* (11 January 1968), Schoenberg's *Erwartung* (Dorothy Dorow), Bax's Third Symphony, Walton's First Symphony, Haydn's *Nelson Mass*, Mendelssohn's *Elijah*, Bartók's *Cantata Profana*, Stravinsky's *Persephone, The Soldier's Tale* and *The Rite of Spring*, Lutoslawski's *Concerto for Orchestra*, Moeran's Violin Concerto, Elgar's *Falstaff*, Frank Martin's *Petite Symphonie Concertante* and a repeat of the McCabe *Variations*. Moshe Atzmon, on 12 October 1967, conducted Bartók's *Music for Strings, Percussion and Celesta*; Hiroyuki Iwaki conducted Webern's *Six Pieces* op. 6 and Prokofiev's Third Symphony; Boult had McCabe as soloist in McCabe's Piano Concerto and conducted Walton's Second Symphony; besides Beethoven and Mozart, Yansons conducted Shostakovich's Eighth and Ninth Symphonies and the Violin Concerto No. 1 (Mikhail Waiman); Charles Groves had a success with Tippett's Second Symphony, and Daniel Barenboim made his Hallé conducting début on 24 March 1968 in Beethoven's 'Eroica' and Schumann's Cello Concerto, with his wife Jacqueline du Pré as soloist. Other soloists were Denis Matthews, John Browning, Ashkenazy (Rachmaninov's Third and Fourth Concertos), Christoph Eschenbach and David Wilde among the pianists, and Szeryng as violinist. Even the guest orchestras were more enterprising in their choice of works, Silvestri conducting the R.L.P.O. in Tchaikovsky's *Manfred* and Menuhin including Britten's *Frank Bridge Variations* and Nicholas Maw's *Sonata for Strings and Two Horns* in the Bath Festival Orchestra's programme. This was surely one of the memorable seasons of the Hallé's history.

If it did not achieve the same heights, the 1968-9 season avoided anti-climax and, of course, each guest conductor was scrutinised as Barbirolli's possible successor. Factions were rife. Barbirolli's contribution was smaller but his programmes were still distinguished, including a Berlioz evening to commemorate the centenary of the composer's death. He conducted Sibelius's Third and Fourth, Shostakovich's Fifth, Mahler's Third and Nielsen's Fifth Symphonies, a programme of Wagner extracts from *Tristan und Isolde* and *Götterdämmerung* with Amy Shuard as solo soprano, Strauss's *Don Quixote*, Ravel's *Shéhérazade* songs with Pauline Stark, Dvořák's Cello Concerto, with Shirley Trepel (a principal cellist in Houston), Brahms's Violin Concerto with Isaac Stern, Berlioz's *Nuits d'Eté* with Margaret Price and the *Symphonie Fantastique,* and Nino Medin's *Serenata Concertante* for viola and double bass, with Ludmilla Navratil and Roy Watson, both Hallé players,[1] as soloists. The main burden of new and unfamiliar works was shouldered by Handford. His programmes included Berlioz's *Requiem, L'Enfance du Christ* (in which there was a lovely performance by the young soprano Annon Lee Silver, who was to die within a short time), and *The Trojans,* performed in two successive weekly parts with a cast headed by Anita Välkki, Anne Pashley, Ann Howard, Bernadette Greevy, Alberto Remedios, Raimund Herincx and Gwynne Howell; Ginastera's First Piano Concerto (Hilde Somer), Rachmaninov's Second Symphony (uncut) and the Third, Scriabin's *Poem of Ecstasy* (neglected since 1923), Thea Musgrave's *Concerto for Orchestra* (15 May), Messiaen's *Oiseaux Exotiques* (Rayson Whalley), Penderecki's *Threnody for the Victims of Hiroshima,* and a concert performance of Verdi's *Aida.* Handford's Berlioz choral concerts were sparsely attended. After *L'Enfance du Christ,* the *Telegraph* critic exasperatedly wrote: 'Need I say that the Manchester public failed to respond to the challenge to listen to some Nativity music besides *Messiah* ? The old faithfuls were there in the Free Trade Hall – some sort of medal ought to be struck for them – but the rest had not come.'

Yansons's extended visit included the usual Tchaikovsky and also Prokofiev's First Violin Concerto (Mikhail Waiman) and Sixth Symphony, Bartók's Second Violin Concerto (Menuhin) and Mozart's *Requiem* (not performed by the Hallé since Hallé's funeral on 29

[1]Miss Navratil was in the orchestra from 1954 to 1962. She left to bring up her children, continuing as a free-lance player. She rejoined the orchestra from 1975 to 1980.

October 1895). There was intense excitement over the three concerts (two programmes) conducted by Carlo Maria Giulini on 7, 10 and 14 November 1968, which included symphonies by Brahms (No. 2) and Mozart (No. 39), Hindemith's *Concert Music*, Mussorgsky's *Pictures from an Exhibition*, two of Debussy's *Nocturnes*, Rossini's *Italian Girl* overture and Casella's *Giara* suite. Moshe Atzmon conducted Bartók's *Miraculous Mandarin* and Hindemith's *Weber Metamorphosis*; Alexander Gibson and Maurice Gendron introduced Britten's great *Cello Symphony* (19 December 1968); a newcomer, the American Lawrence Foster, on 8 December conducted Schumann's Second Symphony and Stravinsky's Concerto for piano and wind (John Ogdon); and David Atherton conducted his first Hallé concert at a Prom on 14 June. But perhaps the most popular guest conductor was Daniel Barenboim. While the Hallé were abroad he came to the Free Trade Hall with the English Chamber Orchestra, with which he had made his conducting début in 1965, in Haydn, Mozart (also playing the solo part in the 27th Piano Concerto) and Bach. Then in March 1969 he conducted a series of concerts with the Hallé, with his friend Ashkenazy as solo pianist in Beethoven's Fourth and Fifth Concertos and the *Choral Fantasia*. He also conducted Beethoven's Seventh and Ninth, Bruckner's Ninth, Haydn's 95th and Schumann's Fourth Symphonies. At the end of the season John Rust resigned as Hallé chorus master. He was succeeded by Raymond Thorpe.

Barenboim also had a major share of the 1969-70 season. He brought two celebrated soloists for their Hallé débuts, Pinchas Zukerman on 12 October in Beethoven's Violin Concerto (he was described by W. R. Sinclair as having 'the physique of a Rugby forward and the technique of a Heifetz') and Alfred Brendel on 22 January 1970 in Bartók's First Piano Concerto. Barenboim conducted Bartók's *Music for Strings, Percussion and Celesta*, Beethoven's G major Concerto with Curzon, Bruckner's Fourth and Seventh Symphonies, and Brahms's Double Concerto with Zukerman and du Pré. At a concert on 15 March to raise money for improvements to the Hallé rehearsal room, he conducted Bruch's G minor Violin Concerto with Zukerman and Elgar's Cello Concerto with du Pré. Of the latter, the *Daily Telegraph* critic wrote that 'her interpretation is a travesty of what it was some years ago. The excessively slow tempi, the exaggerated portamenti, the affected drawing out of one note in a phrase all combined to devalue the great work.' Alas, one could not then know that her every performance was one to treasure, whatever the flaws.

Maurice Handford conducted the first Hallé performances of Vivaldi's *The Four Seasons*, Haydn's *St Nicholas Mass*, Messiaen's *Et*

Exspecto Resurrectionem Mortuorum, Lutoslawski's *Paroles tissées*, Gerhard's *Concerto for Orchestra*, and Webern's *Five Pieces*, op. 10. After the Webern he said to the audience 'You may like to hear those pieces again'. In the words of the *Telegraph* critic, 'no such thought seemed to have occurred to the majority of those present, whose applause had been embarrassingly tepid, but since the work lasts less than five minutes and everybody likes a sporting gesture, they submitted to Mr Handford's will and managed to suppress the coughs that had spluttered through the first playing.' He also conducted Brahms's *Requiem*, Dvořák's *Symphonic Variations*, Bartók's Third Piano Concerto, Stravinsky's *Rite of Spring*, Strauss's *Also sprach Zarathustra*, Hoddinott's Fourth Symphony (its first performance), and a concert performance of Wagner's *Die Meistersinger* on 12 April 1970 with Raimund Herincx as Sachs, Ronald Dowd as Walther, Derek Hammond Stroud as Beckmesser and Margaret Curphey as Eva. There was also a marvellous performance of Elgar's Second Symphony on 4 December of which the *Telegraph* said: 'If this performance had been conducted by, say, Yansons there would have been scenes at the end like the Relief of Mafeking. Yet all the Hallé audience could produce for Mr Handford was a short, cold and perfunctory meed of applause. It was ungenerous, unperceptive and, I suspect, snobbish.' Yansons conducted Shostakovich's 'Leningrad' Symphony (No. 7) and Second Violin Concerto (Boris Gutnikov), Tchaikovsky's *Manfred* and Verdi's *Requiem*. Gibson introduced Henze's Fifth Symphony. Jussi Jalas conducted Nielsen's Violin Concerto (Martin Milner). Boult revived Walton's First Symphony and Beethoven's Triple Concerto, with the Tortelier family as soloists. Lawrence Foster's programmes included the first British performance of Penderecki's *Capriccio* (solo violin Paul Zukofsky), Gunther Schuller's *Seven Studies on Themes of Paul Klee*, Stravinsky's *Jeu de Cartes* (a belated Hallé 'first time') and Webern's *Passacaglia*, op. 1.

Barbirolli's programmes were full of his favourite works. He conducted *Messiah* at Belle Vue at Christmas, with Lenora Lafayette, Helen Watts, Robert Tear and Forbes Robinson; Mahler's Second Symphony; Dvořák's Eighth; Debussy's *La Mer*; Delius's *Appalachia*; Holst's *Planets*; and, to mark his seventieth birthday, Elgar's *Introduction and Allegro*, Vaughan Williams's Sixth and Beethoven's Seventh Symphonies. When he conducted Elgar's First Symphony on 26 October 'some special magic entered the performance,' the *Telegraph* critic wrote, 'and made it not only deeply emotional and moving but seemed to reveal new points of detail and new facets of beauty ... The suppleness of the strings and the superb ensemble of the full orchestra, wholly at one with Barbirolli at his unapproachable best, were exactly in accord with the Elgar ethos . . . Sir John was given a mighty ovation.' For some reason he had never conducted Elgar's *In the South* but he rectified this omission on 30 April 1970, when Gerald Larner called it 'a great performance . . . Sir John phrased the melodies with his very happy instinct for the Elgar line and the Elgar sound.' Barbirolli followed it with Bruckner's Eighth Symphony. On Sunday, 3 May, he conducted Mendelssohn's *Fingal's Cave* and Sibelius's Sixth Symphony, and made a presentation to Arthur Percival, the violinist and brilliant mimic of conductors,[1] who was retiring after thirty-three years in the orchestra, having been its sub-leader from 1943 to 1958. Then he conducted Ravel's *Mother Goose* suite and Stravinsky's *Firebird* suite, with Percival leading the orchestra in the latter work. So at the first desk and on the rostrum were two veterans of the 1943 'miracle'. The audience hailed J. B. as they always did and he waved in his usual way to the side-circle as he walked off for the last time. In Manchester the Barbirolli era had ended.

XIV—*Loughran, 1971-6*

Barbirolli was to have conducted only five Manchester concerts in the 1970-1 season so his death did not necessitate radical revision of the programmes. But he was to have taken the Hallé back to Germany and Austria in November for a fifteen-day tour of Salzburg, Graz, Dornbirn and Innsbruck, and Hanover, Nuremberg, Ludwigshafen, Duisburg and Wuppertal. Instead, Jascha Horenstein conducted eight concerts and Alexander Gibson, conductor of the Scottish National Orchestra, two. Barbirolli would also have enjoyed conducting the celebration in October of the silver jubilee of the foundation of the Hallé Club, of which he had been president for its twenty-five years (he was succeeded by Sir Leonard Behrens). In his place came the conductor of the B.B.C. Scottish Symphony Orchestra, James Loughran, whose interpretation of Beethoven's 'Eroica' Symphony made a deep impression. Two months later, on 16 December, Sir Geoffrey Haworth announced that Loughran would be principal conductor and musical adviser on a three-year contract dating from 1 September 1971.

---

[1] At this little ceremony he gave the audience a sample of his Barbirolli imitation, causing the victim to comment: 'He's more me than I am.' Percival frequently conducted Hallé schools concerts introducing the music with humour and insight. He died in 1973.

Loughran, a Scotsman, was born on 30 June 1931, and educated in Glasgow. He began his conducting career in the opera house, working as a répétiteur with Peter Maag at Bonn Opera, with Netherlands Opera and in Italy. He won the conductors' competition organised by the Philharmonia Orchestra in 1961. From 1962 to 1965 he was associate conductor of the Bournemouth Symphony Orchestra, then went to Glasgow as conductor of the B.B.C. Scottish Symphony Orchestra. He conducted opera at Sadler's Wells in 1963 and at Covent Garden in 1964. He also worked with Scottish Opera and the English Opera Group. His first encounter with the Hallé was, as already stated, in October 1964, and he had conducted it most recently at a Summer Prom on 30 June 1970 when John Lill was soloist with him in Rachmaninov's *Paganini Rhapsody*. As was to be expected, his appointment led to the resignation in April 1971 of Maurice Handford. In his seven years with the Hallé, Handford had conducted many of the most difficult works and had been responsible for the Industrial and Promenade Concerts series. Space precludes detailed mention of these concerts, which are usually 'popular' in design. But Handford injected such delights as a concert performance of Mozart's *Marriage of Figaro* into the Proms schedule. A month after his resignation was announced, he was chosen for the 'Manchester Man of the Year Award', an implied consolation prize but one that was deserved on merit. Readers of the foregoing pages may conclude that if he had felt aggrieved by the Hallé's treatment of him, he could not have been blamed. His last appearance as associate conductor was at the final Prom on 3 July 1971 when he was presented with several Elgar scores by the Society's chairman. The critic W. R. Sinclair commented feelingly on the sense of loss to Manchester of 'so distinguished a musician'.

As it happened, during the 1970-1 season Handford was for once overshadowed in his rôle as chief purveyor of the unusual. Alexander Gibson brought Peter Maxwell Davies's name into the Hallé programmes with the exciting *St Thomas Wake* (22 October). Charles Groves, with the R.L.P.O., conducted Gerhard's Third Symphony ('Collages'). Lawrence Foster, who seemed to be Gerald Larner's choice for the conductorship, conducted the first Hallé performances of Schoenberg's Piano Concerto (Jean-Bernard Pommier, 7 January), Weill's suite from *The Threepenny Opera* (7 January), Alexander Goehr's *Romanza* for cello and orchestra (Siegfried Palm, 21 January) and Ives's *Three Places in New England* (31 January). The most enterprising concert was that on 4 February conducted by Bruno Maderna: Varèse's *Intégrales*, Webern's *Six Pieces*, op. 6, Ligeti's *Atmospheres*, Stravinsky's

Symphony in Three Movements, and his own Violin Concerto (Theo Olof). Another first British performance, like the Maderna concerto, was Kokkonen's Cello Concerto, played by Arto Noras with Jussi Jalas conducting on 18 March. Moshe Atzmon conducted the *Images* of the Israel-domiciled, Hungarian-born Partos and accompanied two great soloists, the violinist Kyung-Wha Chung, new to the Concerts, in the Mendelssohn on 4 October and Alfred Brendel in Mozart's 17th Piano Concerto (K. 453) four days later. At Gibson's concert on 22 October Itzhak Perlman was soloist in Sibelius's Violin Concerto. Handford conducted Vaughan Williams's *Sea Symphony*, a tepid Third Symphony by the American Andrew Imbrie, and Walton's new *Improvisations on an Impromptu of Britten* (29 April). Yansons, besides Russian works in which he excelled, conducted Berg's Violin Concerto (György Pauk). During the season the bicentenary of Beethoven's birth was marked by performances of the nine symphonies, four overtures and four of the five piano concertos.

Other guest conductors were Uri Segal, Jascha Horenstein, Daniel Barenboim on 13 May (Bruckner's Ninth Symphony and Weber's Concerto Fantasie, in a modern edition, with du Pré as solo cellist, her last Manchester appearance), Nicholas Braithwaite, who made his Hallé début at a Prom on 23 June 1971 – and James Loughran, whose appearances in this season had, of course, been booked while Barbirolli was alive. When he walked on to the Free Trade Hall platform on 15 April 1971, news of his appointment was already four months old. He conducted the first Hallé performance of Martinu's Double Concerto for two string orchestras, piano and timpani, Mozart's Piano Concerto No. 12 in A (K. 414) with Christoph Eschenbach, and Bruckner's Sixth Symphony. Desmond Shawe-Taylor attended for the *Sunday Times* and his laudatory review was headed 'Hallé-lujah!' The *Daily Telegraph* critic wrote: 'This concert merely confirmed my view that Mr Loughran is the conductor the Hallé needs. The playing had an urgency and a purpose that we have not heard for 10 months and one sensed an incipient exceptional rapport between orchestra and rostrum'. Four nights later Loughran conducted Berlioz's *Symphonie Fantastique* and the same critic wrote: 'Mr Loughran deserved his first riproaring Manchester ovation . . . It was indeed a very fine and exciting performance . . . different from Barbirolli's in several respects.' In Sheffield a week later he conducted Elgar's *Dream of Gerontius*. It was apparent that Loughran had no inhibitions about succeeding so great and popular a conductor (whom in fact he had never met). 'I realise the enormity of following a man like him,' he told the critic Donald Hanson, 'but I hope it does not sound over-confident if I say that I have no qualms about matching up to the challenge.' The public sensed this attitude and warmed to his personality. Apart from Hallé, who was thirty-eight when he launched his concerts, he was the youngest to hold the Hallé post. His enthusiasm was infectious. He told Gerald Larner that his relationship with the Hallé was 'love at first sight – there was this incredible electricity. It was in Manchester at a Summer Prom [30 June 1970] beginning with Berlioz's *Corsair* overture. I conducted well and they played well. We could have gone on with no rehearsal at all.'

At the concert on 15 April Loughran had performed his first non-musical duty as head of the Hallé family by presenting the twenty-year gold medal to a fellow Scot, the cellist Norah Sandeman. Like his predecessor he did it with charm and with a kiss. Miss Sandeman was the sixth gold medallist in the string section at this date – Eric Davis in the second violins, Donald Shepherd and Audrey Napier Smith in violas, Gladys Yates, principal cellist, and Joseph Richmond, cellist. The five other long-serving members were Charles Cracknell, principal bassoon, Arthur Bevan, horn, Sydney King, trumpet and principal cornet, Terence Nagle, principal trombone, and Rayson Whalley, pianist and percussionist. The other principals were John Adams, viola, Michael Calder, double bass, Roger Rostron, flute, Philip Hill, oboe, James Gregson, clarinet (since 1961), Robert Blackburn, horn, John Dickinson, trumpet, Jack Gledhill, timpani, and Eric Woolliscroft, percussion. Here were experienced players for a new conductor, led by Martin Milner whom Barbirolli had called the finest leader he had ever known.

But if players came and went, the difficult financial situation stayed. Since Yates Lloyd's death in 1969, Rex Hillson had been treasurer and Richard Godlee was deputy chairman to his father-in-law Sir Geoffrey Haworth. The deficit on Barbirolli's last season was £592, making a total deficit of £28,000 in three years. This was in spite of increased assistance from Manchester Corporation. Clive Smart was especially concerned about the average disparity of £1,000 a year between the income expectations of rank-and-file musicians in provincial orchestras and those in London orchestras. In 1971, reporting a deficit of £3,214, Hillson said that inflation had eaten away £30,000 of the Society's reserves in four years. He dismissed the idea that financial salvation lay in greater private patronage. 'The advocates of this solution can have had no experience of raising money for the arts in the regions or they would know that virtually all the available commercial and industrial funds are controlled from London and, with very few notable exceptions, those in authority in London appear to take very little interest in anything happening outside.' Self-help was very much the Hallé's creed (and one very noticeable difference now that Barbirolli had gone was that the management, not the conductor, was the spokesman in times of financial crisis). In 1971 the orchestra played in a Wakefield night club and to any criticism implying a lowering of standards Smart replied: 'A certain £1,000 for an engagement to play standard works is where the conductor and I have to weigh up the balance between what he wants to do musically and what is good business. The very nature of our system of guarantees and grants in this country is that it is more than likely to penalise the financially successful.'

When the programmes for Loughran's first season, 1971-2, were published, they showed no radical departure from the pattern of previous years. The Industrial Concerts were re-named 'Opus 1' and were shared between several conductors instead of being one man's preserve. Loughran conducted in this series and he also appeared at the Manchester Proms, which Barbirolli never had. Loughran continued the Mahler tradition by conducting the Fourth and Fifth Symphonies. The latter was in his first Thursday concert, which opened with Berlioz's *Corsair* and included Musgrave's *Concerto for Orchestra*. Of the Mahler, the *Telegraph*'s critic wrote: 'His grip on the work's structure was strong and his ear for the strands in the texture was sure ... One should never speak of a second Barbirolli or Beecham. The Hallé now have the first Loughran, with all the promise which this concert implied.' He also conducted Elgar's *Falstaff*, Bruckner's Fourth Symphony, the first public performance in Britain of Ligeti's *Lontano* (27 January, 1972), McCabe's song-cycle *Notturni ed Alba* (with Jill Gomez), Holst's *Planets, Messiah* at Belle Vue, John Ogdon's Piano Concerto (composer as soloist), Verdi's *Four Sacred Pieces*, Bartók's *Village Scenes*, with Seefried as soprano soloist, a concert performance of *Aida*, Hindemith's Cello Concerto, Vivaldi's *Gloria*, Mozart's *Vesperae Solennes de Confessore* (K. 339), Goehr's *Little Symphony*, Tippett's *Double Concerto* and several works by Walton to mark the composer's seventieth birthday: the original *Façade* (Polly Elwes and Richard Baker as narrators), the two symphonies, the *Hindemith Variations, Belshazzar's Feast* and the Violin Concerto (Milner). Handford conducted the Cello Concerto (Shirley Trepel) and Paul Doktor played the Viola Concerto with the R.L.P.O. under Groves. New guest conductors included Okko Kamu from Finland (Ives's *Decoration Day*), Edo de Waart, from Holland (Berg's *Three Pieces*, op. 6, and Bartók's Second Piano Concerto), and Rafael Frühbeck de Burgos, from Spain (Falla's *Tricorne*, complete). Horenstein conducted

Nielsen's Sixth Symphony, Pritchard Strauss's *Also sprach Zarathustra*, and Barenboim Elgar's Second Symphony, Brahms's *Requiem* and Busoni's Violin Concerto (Jaime Laredo). He also conducted a Prom. On 31 October Elisabeth Schwarzkopf, against doctor's orders, sang Verdi and Strauss at a concert for the Barbirolli Memorial Foundation which Loughran conducted. Yansons marked Scriabin's centenary with the Second Symphony and also brought the Leningrad Philharmonic to play Shostakovich's Fifth Symphony on 23 September 1971. The Society was 'delighted' to report to its members that Loughran's first season had resulted in a profit of £1,000, the first surplus since 1967. Income from the Free Trade Hall concerts increased by £19,000, breaking all records, and attendance averaged ninety-three per cent of capacity, with more than two-thirds of the concerts sold out. The future, though, like everybody's, was beset by the dread word 'inflation'. Before his next season, Loughran was interviewed for the 1972-3 *Hallé* magazine. What he wanted, he told John Boulton, was a wide representation of styles and periods. He revealed himself as a champion of Schumann, which he conducted 'as written, with none of the Mahlerian alterations or any other changes'. In contemporary music he was 'particularly interested' in Polish and Hungarian composers and in the so-called Manchester School of Maxwell Davies, Goehr and others. He took Stockhausen 'with a great deal of salt'. Questioned about the relative lack of Elgar in his 1972-3 programmes, he replied: 'His music was so associated with John Barbirolli . . . that I thought I should take a year or two before doing many major pieces'. He wanted to do a piece each year by Hindemith – not only was he under-rated, 'but also I *like* his music'.

The 1972-3 season began with a new pattern for the leadership. Martin Milner and Michael Davis were now co-leaders. James Murray, formerly of the B.B.C. Scottish Symphony Orchestra, joined the orchestra to share the first desk of the first violins with whomever was leading. The Hallé Choir had a new chorusmaster in Ronald Frost, director of studies and organ tutor at the Royal Manchester College of Music. He made his 'début' on 8 October in Handel's *Zadok the Priest* and Mozart's 'Coronation' Mass (K. 317).

Of the forty-four Hallé programmes in the season Loughran conducted twenty-three. It was an enterprising season besides needing to observe the centenaries of Vaughan Williams and Rachmaninov. Loughran's concerts included a concert performance of Berlioz's *Beatrice and Benedict* on 4 January in association with the 69 Theatre Company (forerunner of the Royal Exchange Company) to mark Britain's entry into the European Economic Community. The dialogue was spoken by Vanessa Redgrave and Paul Scofield, while the vocal Beatrice and Benedict were Bernadette Greevy and William McAlpine. Loughran also conducted Bruckner's Seventh Symphony, Musgrave's tribute to Beethoven called *Memento Vitae* (23 November, 'compulsive listening', the *Telegraph* critic said), Vaughan Williams's Fifth and Sixth Symphonies, *Serenade to Music*, and Oboe Concerto (with Evelyn Barbirolli), Mahler's *Des Knaben Wunderhorn*, with Janet Baker and the Japanese baritone Eishi Kawamura, Bartók's *Concerto for Orchestra*, Ligeti's *Melodien* (first public performance in Britain on 15 February), Stravinsky's Violin Concerto (Ida Haendel), Holst's *Egdon Heath* (almost certainly its first Hallé performance, at a Prom on 30 June), Robert Simpson's Fourth Symphony (dedicated to Loughran, 'my friend and fellow Beethovenian') on 26 April 1973, Hindemith's *Concert Music*, Britten's *Les Illuminations* (Elisabeth Robinson) and Verdi's *Requiem*.

Of the guest conductors, Efrem Kurtz conducted Hindemith's *Nobilissima Visione*, and Roussel's Third Symphony; Yansons, criticised for too much predictable Tchaikovsky, brought Emil Gilels to play the First Piano Concerto (12 November). Gilels unfolded it, Sinclair wrote, 'as a perfect combination of the lyrical and dramatic'. Yansons also conducted Shostakovich's Sixth Symphony (9 November). There was high critical praise for Istvan Kertesz, whose programmes included Bartók's Second Violin Concerto (Eszter Perényi), Mahler's *Rückertlieder* (Yvonne Minton), and Dvořák's Sixth Symphony, neglected by the Hallé since 1886. The audience's ovation for him, the *Telegraph* critic wrote, meant 'Come back soon'. Alas, Kertesz was to die by drowning four months later. Hiroyuki Iwaki conducted Takemitsu's *Textures* and Nielsen's Fifth Symphony; Meredith Davies introduced Vaughan Williams's *Dona Nobis Pacem* to Manchester thirty-six years after the Hallé had taken part in its first performance in Huddersfield, and Sir Adrian Boult revived Parry's *Symphonic Variations* and conducted Vaughan Williams's *London Symphony* ('a Regent Street interpretation compared with Barbirolli's Cockney', the *Telegraph* critic said). Frühbeck de Burgos, Lawrence Foster and Okko Kamu (Prokofiev Seventh Symphony) also returned. At the Prom on 22 June, Andrew Davis made his début as Hallé guest conductor and 'early music' came to the concerts on 28 June when the Early Music Consort of London, directed by the lamented David Munrow, performed Renaissance works by Monteverdi, Gabrieli and others.

Towards the end of the season, in May 1973, the Hallé faced a deficit by the end of the year of over £68,000 because of rapidly rising costs and the incidence of the new Value Added Tax. A projected ten per cent increase in ticket prices for 1973-4 was not expected to make much difference because of a consequent drop in attendances. Manchester City Council at once, and without debate, raised its direct grant to the Hallé by ten per cent to a total of £61,000 and also gave £12,000 to the regional scheme to aid the Hallé and R.L.P.O. As a result the situation was contained, mainly because concert income exceeded £250,000 for the first time. From 1974 Hallé assistance also came from the Greater Manchester County Council, formed as a result of what many people regard as the inflationary and unnecessary reorganisation of local government. In its first year, G.M.C. voted a £75,000 grant to the Hallé, with a further £35,000 guarantee to offset any shortfall in grants from other authorities. The City Council continued to aid the Hallé to the tune of £30,000 because it retained power to vote money to organisations which specifically benefited the city. Before the start of Loughran's third season, 1973-4, the Society announced that he was to continue as principal conductor at least until 1976 and probably beyond. The Free Trade Hall season began with a gala concert in aid of the Trust Fund, with Geza Anda as solo pianist in Beethoven's C minor concerto. At the opening Thursday concert, Loughran conducted the contemporary Czech composer Luboš Fišer's *Fifteen Prints of Dürer's Apocalypse* and Bruckner's Sixth Symphony. Later in the season he conducted Bliss's Piano Concerto (Clive Lythgoe), Prokofiev's Fifth Symphony, Lutoslawski's *Concerto for Orchestra*, Tchaikovsky's Second Symphony, Berg's *Altenbergleider* (Heather Harper), the first performance of Stephen Dodgson's Second Guitar Concerto (John Williams), McCabe's *Hartmann Variations*, Britten's *Serenade* (with Robert Tear, tenor, and the Hallé's principal horn since 1973, Michael Purton), Hindemith's *Mathis der Maler* Symphony and two performances which merit fuller mention. On 7 March he conducted Elgar's First Symphony, thus, to quote the *Telegraph* critic, 'exorcising for himself the ghost of his predecessor . . . His interpretation is so different from Sir John Barbirolli's that no question of comparison arises, odious or otherwise. Whereas Sir John's Elgar trailed clouds of Elgarian, Edwardian and his own glory, Mr Loughran's is more concerned with the brilliant orchestrator than the subtly complex tone-poet . . . He was giving us an historical view of Elgar, the view of a generation which has not touched the hem of Sir Edward's robe.' On 2 May a triumphant performance of Beethoven's Choral Symphony inspired a leader in the *Manchester Evening News* proclaiming the reality of the Loughran era.

In place of Bruno Maderna, Maurice Handford returned to conduct

(7 October) Maderna's *Biogramma* and Boulez's *Improvisations sur Mallarmé*; Boult conducted Elgar's Second Symphony – memorably – on 5 May 1974 to mark his own eighty-fifth birthday. This was to prove to be his last Hallé appearance. Britten's sixtieth birthday was saluted by the *War Requiem*, conducted by Meredith Davies. Kurtz, Yansons (with Shostakovich's Fifteenth Symphony) and Atzmon were also among the guest conductors. John Pritchard conducted Ives's Fourth Symphony, a centenary tribute which estranged many of the audience, and Lawrence Foster conducted Mahler's Seventh Symphony on 25 October, a performance described by Larner as 'carefully prepared and well finished'. He praised individual sections of the orchestra, 'but the most moving aspect of all was the unanimity and beauty of the violin playing and the wonderful clarity throughout the whole orchestral texture'. Of the conductor he wrote: 'Mr Foster was not working for orchestral brilliance at Mahler's expense. It was an utterly sincere and genuine interpretation, as extrovert only as it need be . . . The Hallé Orchestra recognised these qualities and collaborated with all the skill, taste and imagination at its disposal – which, it has at last revealed, is more than a little.' Peter Maag and Owain Arwel Hughes were among the newcomers to the Hallé rostrum. New names appeared among the soloists during this period: pianists such as Radu Lupu, Rafael Orozco, Tamas Vásary, Imogen Cooper, Paul Crossley, Howard Shelley, Walter Klien and Cristina Ortiz. Both Zukerman and Perlman were solo violinists during the season, but they were about to move into a stratosphere where the Hallé could no longer reach them. Manchester may have been on the 'superstar' circuit in 1836, but 1974 was another matter. At the Proms there were two unusual events: the concert by Grimethorpe Colliery Band and the Hallé Choir under Elgar Howarth which included David Bedford's *Star Clusters, Nebulae and Places in Devon*, and Loris Tjeknavorian's first appearance as composer-conductor, in a programme including the first British performance of his Piano Concerto, played by David Wilde. 'The most notable thing about this piece,' wrote Paul Dewhirst of the *Daily Telegraph*, 'was surely how much of the groundwork had been done by Bartók in his First Piano Concerto of 1926.'

Attendance at the Thursday series in Manchester in 1973-4 was ninety-eight per cent, the Sunday series ninety-five per cent, the Proms ninety-five per cent and Opus 1 a hundred per cent. Membership of the Society in 1974 reached the record figure of 2,500. When Loughran was appointed in 1971, there had been 1,500 members. It seemed a trifle ungracious, therefore, of one of these members to complain at the 1973 annual meeting that the orchestra

James Loughran (*above*) rehearsing in April 1971 for his first Hallé concert after his appointment as principal conductor. *Below*: a Hallé social occasion. *Left to right, front*: Lady and Sir Leonard Behrens, Richard Godlee; *back*: James Loughran, Eslyn Kennedy, Sir Geoffrey Haworth, Michael Kennedy, Lady Haworth, Harold Riley, Nancy Loughran

James Loughran on the rostrum and in the recording playback studio, with John Boyden (*left*) and Martin Milner

played better for visiting conductors and that players were leaving because of severe working conditions and 'also apparently because of the not very satisfactory atmosphere with the conductor'. Sir Geoffrey Haworth said such criticism was unjustified. Standards of playing had improved. 'During the last year or two of Sir John's time with the orchestra, his name and reputation were masking what I think were certain orchestral difficulties.' The working conditions were alleviated from 1 April 1974 by a pay increase which gave experienced rank-and-file players a basic £50 a week (an increase of £7), and a forty-hour week divided into twenty-five hours playing time and fifteen travelling. Since 1958, there had been a determined attempt to improve the orchestra's conditions of work. Smart chose the start of Loughran's renewed contract to launch a drive for £25,000 a year of extra industrial and commercial sponsorship. 'We are not going round with our begging bowl,' he said, 'we have a gilt-edged product to sell. The 1974-5 season is the take-off point at which the Hallé, which attained an international reputation under Barbirolli, will again move ahead and achieve new peaks of greatness under James Loughran.'

A welcome announcement was the Hallé's return to the recording studio, from which it had been absent since Sir John's death. The Hallé had left H.M.V. in 1954 and recorded for Pye from 1955 to 1960. From 1964 (with Elgar's Second Symphony) it returned to H.M.V. Now it rejoined E.M.I. on the Classics for Pleasure label. The first Hallé–Loughran recording – of Rachmaninov's Second Symphony – was issued in September 1974. Alan Blyth, in the *Hallé* magazine, wrote that it 'seems to show off, almost flawlessly, the orchestra's new-found strength . . . What I very much admired was the rich string tone.' The London critics at this time were more favourable to Loughran's Hallé than they had often been to Barbirolli's and more favourable than most of the Manchester critics. This is perhaps not surprising, for 'local' critics are inclined to be harder on the home side, which they see (hear) more often. And the Hallé no doubt tends to find a bit extra for London, where it knows it will be compared with the four metropolitan orchestras. Nevertheless the London and Manchester critics of the *Daily Telegraph* were unanimous about the performances of the Rachmaninov symphony which started the Hallé's 1974-5 season in each city. 'Magnificent interpretation . . . resplendent and assured performance,' the Northern critic wrote, while Martin Cooper at the Festival Hall singled out the strings' 'handsome, full-bodied tone and beautifully sustained line, whilst the clarinet solo [James Gregson] at the opening of the adagio held the audience spellbound by its perfect control and modulation of phrase and dynamics'. Of the Manchester concert on 3 October at which Loughran conducted works by the season's centenarians, Ives, Holst and Schoenberg (Violin Concerto, Zvi Zeitlin), the *Telegraph* critic wrote that it 'was testimony to the rapidly maturing powers of Mr Loughran, of which one has never been in doubt. Manchester, if the place runs true to form, will be the last to notice.'

During this 1974-5 season Hallé performances were given of Ives's *Three Places in New England* and *The Unanswered Question*, Prokofiev's Fourth Symphony (Foster), Maki Ishii's *Kyo-so* (Iwaki), Tcherepnin's Sixth Piano Concerto (Ogdon), Tippett's First Symphony (Groves and R.L.P.O.) and Piano Concerto (Paul Crossley and Andrew Davis), and Havergal Brian's Tenth Symphony (Loughran). Loughran also conducted several contemporary British works: Musgrave's Viola Concerto (Peter Mark), Thomas Wilson's *Threnody*, Goehr's *Sonata about Jerusalem*, Gordon Crosse's *Memories of Morning, Night*, and the first public performance of a Hallé commission, John McCabe's *The Chagall Windows* (9 January 1975; the Hallé had already recorded the work). During the season Victoria de los Angeles sang Falla; Owain Arwel Hughes conducted Holst's *Choral Symphony*; Yansons repeated Shostakovich's Fifteenth Symphony and introduced the fourth ('He has had no greater artistic triumph in his decade as a Hallé guest conductor than this superlative performance', the *Telegraph* critic wrote); Loughran conducted two Bruckner symphonies, the Fourth and Eighth. After the latter, Gerald Larner wrote in the *Guardian* that 'one fact was clear: James Loughran is now fully accepted by the Hallé Orchestra as its rightful conductor. No one who had not won its complete confidence would have got such a committed performance of such sustained intensity as he did . . . a performance of such general orchestral distinction and such emotional upheaval.' Loughran also conducted Mahler's *Das Lied von der Erde*, with Janet Baker and John Mitchinson, a critic writing of Baker that 'in her voice at present the soul of whatever music she is singing seems to be enshrined'. Larner said of this performance that 'at his best Mr Loughran forgets the audience behind him, loses the conductor self-consciousness, ignores the stylish image . . . he gives himself completely to the music, taking the orchestra all the way with him'. Bela Siki played Bartók's Second Piano Concerto. Claudio Arrau and Clifford Curzon played Brahms's First Piano Concerto; Lukas Foss conducted his own *Baroque Variations* (boos and cheers at the end); John Pritchard conducted Rachmaninov's *The Bells*, Szymanowski's First Violin Concerto (Wanda Wilkomirska) and Mahler's First Symphony, which served appositely as a memorial tribute to Sir Neville Cardus, who had died a week earlier on 28

February 1975; Handford conducted Elgar's *The Apostles*; and Alfred Brendel was solo pianist in Beethoven's C minor concerto. In January 1975 Loughran took the Hallé to Germany and Switzerland for an eighteen-day tour, playing in Ludwigshafen, Nuremberg, Würzburg, Kassel, Hanover, Kiel, Goslar and Heidelberg, and Lausanne, Basle, Berne and Zürich. Clifford Curzon and Ulf Hoelscher travelled as piano and violin soloists. Among the works played were Beethoven's Fourth and Brahms's First Piano Concertos, Mendelssohn's Violin Concerto and Elgar's First Symphony.

The 1975-6 season had a special significance because for the first time since the days of Brand Lane the Hallé encountered rival public orchestral concerts in the Free Trade Hall. The enlarged B.B.C. Northern Symphony Orchestra, under its then principal conductor, Raymond Leppard, inaugurated an annual series of six Master Concerts, given monthly from October to March, which soon became a valuable feature of Manchester's musical life. With B.B.C. finance behind them, these concerts at the start had very enterprising programmes. The orchestra, too, with ampler rehearsal conditions, achieved superb playing in many of the nineteenth-century classics regarded as prime Hallé territory. Such competition can only be healthy for artistic standards. The Manchester public, increasingly loath, it seemed, to vary its diet or to try new dishes, stayed away from the B.B.C. concerts in multitudes. With the advent of the Royal Northern College of Music as a major centre of musical activities, the demands on the music lover's purse, at a time of increasing inflation, enforced selectiveness of choice. If one had bought a Hallé subscription ticket, then spare cash for concert-going was likely to be spent on recitals rather than on another set of orchestral concerts.

Loughran's programmes for 1975-6 included Nicholas Maw's immediately attractive *Scenes and Arias*, Britten's Piano Concerto (Ogdon), Mahler's Third and Fifth Symphonies, Bruckner's Second Symphony, Elgar's Second Symphony (8 April), Shostakovich's Fifth Symphony, Bartók's Viola Concerto (Max Rostal),[1] Don Banks's *Prospects* and Vivaldi's *Gloria*. He conducted concertos for Tortelier, Annie Fischer, Arrau and Katin. The season's biggest adventures were Ligeti's Cello Concerto (22 April), played by Vladimir Orloff and conducted by an American newcomer, James Conlon, and Lutoslawski's Second Symphony (26 February) under Stanislaw Skrowaczewski from Minnesota. Neither work was generally liked.

[1] William Primrose, the Hallé and Barbirolli gave this work its first British performance at the 1950 Edinburgh Festival but did not play it in Manchester.

Nor was Florent Schmitt's *Psalm 47*, conducted by Pritchard. Gibson conducted Vaughan Williams's Ninth Symphony, Kurtz Prokofiev's Second, Yansons Shostakovich's Eleventh, Ždenek Macal Strauss's *Also sprach Zarathustra* and Okko Kamu Haydn's *The Creation*. Solo recitals were given a prominent place in the scheme – by the singers Elisabeth Schwarzkopf and Dame Janet Baker and the guitarists Segovia and Narciso Yepes. There were also more guest orchestras than usual – a Bach evening by the German Bach Soloists, Haitink and the London Philharmonic in Bruckner's Eighth Symphony (Larner wrote of this that he 'preferred James Loughran's interpretation. . . but even the most loyal Hallé supporters would have to admit that the L.P.O. has a superbly cohesive sound'), Groves and the R.L.P.O., Louis Frémaux and the City of Birmingham Symphony Orchestra (Tippett's *Fantasia Concertante on a Theme of Corelli* and Saint-Saëns's Third Symphony), and Albert Rosen and the Radio Telefis Eireann Symphony Orchestra in Mahler's First Symphony. The Hallé was away from England in February 1976 when it gave eleven concerts at the fourth Hong Kong Festival. The programmes included the 'plums' of the Hallé repertoire and were enthusiastically received, the leading critic writing of 'performances that grip the heart and will not let go'. Loughran conducted six concerts, including a Viennese Evening, the other five being conducted by Meredith Davies and Owain Arwel Hughes. The soloists were Moura Lympany and Peter Katin (pianists), Stoika Milanova (violin) and, in an operatic programme, the singers Valerie Masterson, Patricia Kern and Christian du Plessis. Outside the concert-hall, the Hallé's golf team lost its match, and the ten members of the orchestra who took part in sailing races also lost! Working in Hong Kong was Captain Bruce Micklewright, who had been made an honorary member of the Hallé after being co-pilot of the orchestra's chartered aircraft on its South American tour in 1968. He gave a supper party for those players and officials – over thirty of them – who had been on the earlier tour. When the Hallé returned to Hong Kong five years later, Captain Micklewright was still there to greet it.

So Loughran's first five years ended with a profit on the 1975-6 season of over £10,000. The orchestra's earned income was still spectacularly high, increasing by nearly forty per cent to £433,455, and this in spite of a thirty per cent increase in ticket prices. Of subsidisers, the Arts Council was the largest, with £175,000 plus a £10,000 guarantee against loss. G.M.C. gave £125,000 and a £15,000 guarantee. Both these organisations had increased their aid since 1974-5 by twenty-three per cent and twenty-seven per cent respectively. Manchester City Council's grant stayed unchanged at

£30,000, of which a substantial amount was recouped by the city in rent (recently increased by fifty per cent) for the Free Trade Hall.

Two deaths in the first weeks of 1976 broke famous Hallé links. Rayson Whalley, the orchestra's pianist and a member of the percussion section since 1948, was taken ill just before the Hong Kong tour and died suddenly. Kindly, witty and extremely knowledgeable about music (not the case with every orchestral player), he was a brilliant musician whose feat in playing Vaughan Williams's *Sinfonia Antartica* at sight from the manuscript won the composer's astonished admiration in 1952. On 21 January the former leader, Laurance Turner, died. His services to music in Manchester extended beyond the Hallé, in which he had first played in 1920 and which he led for eighteen years. His quartet gave the city's most enterprising chamber concerts; it played all the Bartók quartets in 1949 when other organisations were still terrified of them. With Lucy Pierce, he gave frequent sonata recitals and, after leaving the Hallé, he directed the Manchester Mid-day Concerts from 1954 to 1972, giving many a young artist a valuable opportunity to launch a career. He was modest and self-effacing to an extraordinary degree; he never grumbled and he worked very hard. He, let it never be forgotten, suggested to Godlee and Forbes that Barbirolli was the conductor they needed. With his quiet temperament, he complemented ideally Barbirolli's Latin emotionalism. They respected and liked each other, Barbirolli often referring to Turner as 'the rock' on which he could rely. But no tribute to Laurance Turner would be complete which did not mention his passionate devotion to all animals, from lions to poodles with plenty in between. There is a delightful story of a rehearsal of the finale of Mahler's Ninth Symphony. As the music drew to its halting, tragic close, Barbirolli noticed tears glistening in his leader's eyes. 'Yes, it's terribly moving, isn't it?' J.B. said gently, to which Laurance replied: 'It's not the music, John. Our cat died this morning.'

XV—*Loughran, 1976-83*

The 1976-7 season began with James Loughran conducting Shostakovich's Tenth Symphony, but the 'official' Hallé memorial concert for the Russian composer, who had died the previous year, was fittingly conducted by Arvid Yansons. He selected two major works, the First Violin Concerto (Arve Tellefsen) and the Seventh ('Leningrad') Symphony, both of which have been among the strongest interpretations by the Hallé's chief guest conductor. Loughran conducted three Mahler symphonies, the Fourth, Fifth and Ninth, the last on 12 May 1977. He also concentrated on British composers: Elgar's Cello Concerto (Joan Dickson), Second Symphony and *The Dream of Gerontius* (22 May, with Janet Baker, Philip Langridge and Michael Rippon), Vaughan Williams's Sixth Symphony, a Walton seventy-fifth birthday evening containing both symphonies and the Violin Concerto (Aaron Rosand) on 14 April, and works by two other living composers, William Mathias's *Laudi* and Gordon Crosse's *Some Marches on a Ground*. Three Delius works were in the care of guest conductors: the *Mass of Life* (20 February, Handford; 'where it mattered most, in the last 30 minutes, Mr Handford got everything together and the spell was cast – a magical spell, unique of its kind', the *Telegraph* critic wrote); *Sea-Drift* (Pritchard); and *Paris* (Edward Downes). Handford conducted Schoenberg's *Pelleas and Melisande* and a concert version of Gershwin's *Porgy and Bess*, and other Loughran performances included Schumann's Cello Concerto (Tortelier), Nielsen's Violin Concerto (Milner), Sibelius's Fourth Symphony, Bartók's *Kossuth* (its first Hallé performance since 1904), Tchaikovsky's *Manfred*, Ravel's *L'Enfant et les Sortilèges*, and plenty of Beethoven. Paul Dewhirst, in *The Daily Telegraph*, summed up Loughran's virtues in Beethoven when writing of a 'superb account' of the Seventh Symphony on 2 January 1977: 'The great strength . . . lay in the conductor's ability to take the overall view, both of individual movements and of the entire symphony . . . The rhythmic drive and control never faltered.' (Richard Osborne, reviewing the Hallé recording of the 'Eroica' in *Gramophone*, wrote of Loughran's Beethoven as 'already complex, emergently great . . . Time and again Loughran's integrity and his fine sense of detail lead him to unearth points of structure, points of drama and points of beauty which make for genuinely fascinating Beethoven interpretation.')

During the season Yansons conducted Bruckner's Third Symphony, Pritchard Nielsen's Fourth, Efrem Kurtz Stravinsky's *Symphony of Psalms*, Ole Schmidt Nielsen's Second Symphony, Gunther Schuller his own Violin Concerto (Zvi Zeitlin), Leonard Slatkin *Moby Dick* by Peter Mennin, and Walter Süsskind Berg's Chamber Concerto. Among the new guest conductors were Hans Vonk and Pinchas Steinberg. There were piano recitals by Barenboim and Ashkenazy, chamber concerts (mainly Bach) by the Zagreb Soloists, with James Galway as director and solo flautist, and the Leipzig Gewandhaus Bach Orchestra and, on 28 November 1976, to mark the twenty-fifth anniversary of the re-opening of the Free Trade Hall, a return visit by

126

the hall's first guest orchestra, the Hamburg Radio Orchestra, now re-titled Norddeutsche Rundfunk Symphony Orchestra, under Moshe Atzmon. Its performance of Brahms's First Symphony was described by W. R. Sinclair as 'typically Germanic'. The season's soloists included Rudolf Serkin, Ilana Vered, Gina Bachauer, Michael Roll, Walter Klien, John Lill, Anthony Goldstone, Imogen Cooper, Murray Perahia, Cristina Ortiz, and Jean-Bernard Pommier among pianists, Kyung-Wha Chung, Mark Kaplan, György Pauk and Michael Davis among violinists, and a galaxy of singers from Sheila Armstrong, Elizabeth Harwood, Margaret Marshall, Janet Baker and Sandra Browne to Richard Lewis, Gwynne Howell and Raimund Herincx. In January 1977 the Hallé and Loughran returned to Switzerland to play in Basle, Berne, Geneva, Lausanne and Zürich. In each city the programme was Beethoven's Fourth Piano Concerto (John Lill) and Bruckner's Fourth Symphony.

The Hallé's surplus on the year 1976-7 was £33,643, small enough on a turnover of over £1 million but with the orchestra earning sixty per cent of its financial needs. Nothing could have provided a happier culmination to the thirteen-year chairmanship of Sir Geoffrey Haworth, who retired at the end of 1977 but remained on the committee. (This remarkable octogenarian then threw all his considerable energy into chairmanship, and later presidency, of the trust which administered the lavish and courageous refurbishment of the Palace Theatre.) He was succeeded by the treasurer, Rex Hillson, a member of the committee since September 1948, who, in the *Hallé* magazine, gave his aspirations as 'a radical improvement in the working conditions of the orchestra', a concert-hall in Manchester, better rehearsal accommodation, and a tour of America. Disenchantment with the Free Trade Hall was now rife. Not only was it expensive for the Society, it was uncomfortable for the public. What had seemed acceptable in the austerity-England of 1951 now appeared as shoddy makeshift. Compared with the comfort of new concert-halls elsewhere, the Free Trade Hall was found increasingly wanting.

Although the Hallé programmes were at this time severely criticised for their conservative approach and for their predictability – Gerald Larner's joke was that they were produced by a computer in the Hallé's Cross Street offices – the 120th season (1977-8) was by no means unadventurous. There had been alarm about the new policy, dictated by economic necessity, whereby certain works played on a Thursday were to be repeated on the following Sunday. Britten, who had died in December 1976, was commemorated by his *Suite on English Folk Tunes*, the *Cantata Academica* and the *Cantata Misericordium*. The first Hallé (but

127

not Manchester) performance of Shostakovich's Fourteenth Symphony (Yansons, 27 April 1978) was an indirect tribute, since the work is dedicated to Britten. Yansons also conducted the Sixth Symphony and Loughran the Tenth. Stravinsky was well represented: *Petrushka* (Okko Kamu), the *Capriccio* for piano (soloist Michel Beroff), the Concerto for piano and wind (soloist Claude Helffer, conductor Michel Tabachnik), and the *Little Suite No. 2*, conducted by Yuri Ahronovich. Loughran conducted Elgar's First and Bruckner's Eighth Symphonies, Kurt Weill's Violin Concerto (Karl-Ove Mannberg), Beethoven's Mass in C, *Messiah*, Strauss's *Ein Heldenleben*, Sándor Balassa's *Iris*, the first performance of Gordon Crosse's *Play Ground* (a Hallé commission), Wagner's *Wesendonck Songs* (Janet Baker) and the first Manchester performance of David Blake's Violin Concerto (Iona Brown), a work which the *Telegraph* critic said 'springs from deep impulses . . . and we are moved by the way Blake was moved'. Tabachnik conducted the Hallé's first Xenakis, his *Eridanos*, on 27 October 1977 ('sound-patterns well on the way to being outmoded', the *Telegraph* critic decided), Kamu brought Sallinen's Cello Concerto (Arto Noras), Owain Arwel Hughes conducted Prokofiev's cantata *Alexander Nevsky*, and there was a newcomer, Guido Ajmone-Marsan. Of the guest orchestras, Previn and the L.S.O. strongly challenged the home team in Rachmaninov's Second Symphony, Haitink conducted the L.P.O. in Elgar's Second Symphony, Michael Tilson Thomas conducted the London Sinfonietta in the first performance of Simon Bainbridge's Viola Concerto (Walter Trampler, 12 March 1978) and Renato Fasano and the Virtuosi di Roma gave a Vivaldi programme including *The Four Seasons*. With soloists like Brendel, Szeryng, John Lill, Radu Lupu and Heinrich Schiff (cello), there was also room for two young Englishmen. Here is Paul Dewhirst of the *Daily Telegraph* first on the violinist Nigel Kennedy (3 May 1978) in Bruch's G minor concerto: '(He) seemed to go straight to the heart of the music with his "inward" yet expressive playing'; and secondly on the cellist Colin Carr in Elgar's concerto (22 February 1978): 'Mr Carr is already well inside this very testing work . . . His playing is not intrusively personal in the slightly self-indulgent way of some cellists.' As in previous and subsequent seasons, the pre-concert talks organised on Thursdays by Barbara Fleming of Manchester University Extra-Mural Department were a valuable way of stimulating interest in the programmes.

Before the 1977-8 season began, Loughran had announced his appointment as chief conductor of the Bamberg Symphony Orchestra from September 1979, following the pattern set by Barbirolli and Houston. Charles Cracknell M.B.E., principal bassoonist since 1946, retired because of ill-health in the spring of 1978, and on 12 March Sir Leonard Behrens died at the age of eighty-seven. Behrens had first joined the Hallé Committee in 1932, later becoming treasurer and chairman. When he retired from the committee in 1974 he had been made an honorary member for life. For over thirty years he was on the Council of the Royal Manchester College of Music and was a member for many years of the University Council. He was also a former president of the Liberal Party and a vice-president of the United Nations Association. Even when it became unfashionable, he believed in the importance of Manchester. He enjoyed controversy and he alienated some people – Barbirolli among them – by what they deemed his wrongheadedness or his facetious tactlessness. But he was not devious and he remained on good terms with most of his opponents. At their home in Didsbury he and his wife regularly gathered together people from a wide cross-section of Manchester's life. In this respect he was following his family's tradition. He once signed a letter 'yours ever in the service of civilisation'. That was his greatness. In the context of the city as it used to be, he was perhaps the last great Mancunian.

The 1978-9 season began with the presentation of twenty-year gold medals to the leader Martin Milner and to the general manager, Clive Smart, the first administrator to receive it. Stuart Robinson, the genial and ever-helpful concerts manager since he joined the Society in 1961 at the age of twenty-four, was appointed deputy general manager. He received his medal in the 1980-1 season. The programmes were alarmingly cautious, audiences having declined during 1977-8, and there was criticism among the more enlightened concert-goers of the absence of works by Maxwell Davies, Birtwistle and Maw among English composers and by Berio, Boulez, Penderecki and Elliott Carter among foreign contemporaries. Loughran's Bamberg commitments meant that he conducted only six of the sixteen Thursday concerts and six of the fifteen Sunday series. Works he conducted included Lutoslawski's *Mi-Parti* (2 November 1978), McCabe's *Hartmann Variations*, Strauss's *Don Quixote* (with the Hallé principal cellist Peter Worrall a superb soloist), Mahler's Sixth Symphony, Elgar's Second Symphony, Beethoven's Ninth, and Bartók's *Music for Strings, Percussion and Celesta*. Soloists appearing with him were Arrau, Ashkenazy, Foldes, and Menuhin. Among the guest conductors, Vernon Handley again earned praise for his adoption of the Boult system of dividing first and second violins, Karsten Andersen was on the rostrum for an unprovoked assault on Rachmaninov's D minor piano concerto by Roger Woodward, Iosif Conta conducted Stravinsky's *Rite of Spring*, and Atzmon conducted the first Hallé performance of Bruckner's Fifth Symphony (22 March 1979). Highest critical praise was reserved for Kurt Sanderling (19 April) who, a *Telegraph* writer said, gave a lesson 'in that magical art whereby a conductor, after only a few rehearsals, can change an orchestra's style and impose his artistry upon it . . . Who could believe, listening to the rhythmic precision and superb dead-on-the-beat response in Stravinsky's *Symphony in Three Movements* that this was the orchestra which so often mars its warm and heartfelt playing with ragged entries and sloppy rhythms? . . . Could Mr Sanderling keep it up in Schumann's Fourth Symphony; more important, could the Hallé? Yes, they could and did.' The same writer revelled in Yansons's interpretation of Mahler's Second Symphony on 5 April – 'the audience directed its tremendous ovation to Mr Yansons and it was right to do so'. Yansons's son, Mariss, had made a strong impression in Prokofiev, Tchaikovsky and Sibelius when he conducted the Leningrad Philharmonic in Manchester on 8 October 1979. Previn conducted the L.S.O. in Vaughan Williams's *London Symphony*, Iona Brown directed the Academy of St Martin-in-the-Fields in Bach and Vivaldi, and Lawrence Foster conducted the R.L.P.O. in the first Hallé performance of Shostakovich's Thirteenth Symphony, with Willard White as the bass soloist, on 22 February.

These visits were while Loughran and the Hallé made two foreign tours, in November 1978 to Norway and Sweden, giving five concerts, each including Dvořák's Eighth Symphony, and in February 1979 to Germany where thirteen concerts were given in fifteen days in Stuttgart, Augsburg, Munich, Regensburg, Nuremberg, Bonn, Oberhausen, Wuppertal, Bielefeld, Osnabrück, Kassel, Brunswick and Berlin. Bad weather made travelling extremely perilous, but every venue was reached in time. The repertoire included Brahms's Fourth Symphony, Britten's *Young Person's Guide to the Orchestra*, Dvořák's Eighth Symphony (nine performances), McCabe's *Hartmann Variations*, and Tippett's Suite in D. In six performances of Brahms's Double Concerto, Ulf Hoelscher and David Geringas were the violin and cello soloists, André Watts played Beethoven's Fourth Piano Concerto and, when the orchestra played in the Philharmonic Hall, Berlin, Wolfgang Schneiderhan joined it in Brahms's Violin Concerto. There had been new names among the Manchester soloists – the cellist Yo Yo Ma, the violinists Lydia Mordkovitch and Mayumi Fujikawa – but one is especially poignant. The English pianist Terence Judd played Rachmaninov's Second Concerto on 10 December 1978. W. R. Sinclair declared that 'already it would seem he stands at the head of a small group of greatly gifted young British pianists, and even in so familiar a work managed to impart a degree of freshness'. Within a year Judd was dead, aged twenty-two.

During the summer of 1979 the Hallé lost the services of its co-leader, Michael Davis, who became leader of the London Symphony Orchestra. His successor was the thirty-year-old leader of the Ulster Orchestra, Pan Hon Lee, who was born in Singapore of Chinese parents. He was a pupil of Sidney Griller and Szymon Goldberg and also studied in Bucharest. He made his first appearance in Manchester on 20 December 1979. The orchestra played at the Cheltenham Festival, where under Sir Charles Groves it played Berkeley's Third Symphony and under Elgar Howarth gave the first performance of Gordon Crosse's Cello Concerto (soloist, Rohan de Sarem). The concerto was repeated at a Prom in Manchester a few days later, on 10 July 1979. At the Edinburgh Festival on 3 September, Loughran conducted the Hallé in the first performance of Richard Rodney Bennett's *Sonnets for Orpheus*, for cello (Heinrich Schiff) and orchestra. Alan Blyth, in the *Daily Telegraph*, called it 'a major addition to the Bennett canon'. It was repeated twice in Manchester in the 1979-80 programmes, which received a more enthusiastic welcome from the critics (for whom, as Hallé Committee members like to point out, programmes are not designed), one of them having described 1978-9 as 'the least important and most easily forgettable Hallé season for years'. Entry into the Free Trade Hall in September 1979 to hear, yet again, John Lill and Loughran in a Brahms piano concerto was subtly different, however, because of the announcement in the previous June of plans to convert the Victorian Refuge Assurance building on Oxford Street into an arts complex. Raymond Slater, mastermind of the refurbished Palace Theatre, was at the heart of this new project. The only new building required, he said, would be a concert-hall for the Hallé. Rex Hillson, the Hallé chairman, firmly supported the plan; if it becomes reality, its importance for the Hallé needs no underlining.

In the 1979-80 season Loughran conducted Mahler's Third and Fifth Symphonies, Bruckner's Seventh, Schoenberg's *Variations* of 1928 (its first Manchester performance, on 17 January 1980), Hindemith's *Mathis der Maler*, Harty's Violin Concerto (Ralph Holmes) and Berlioz's *Symphonie Fantastique* (both to mark Harty's centenary), Beethoven's Triple Concerto (Beaux Arts Trio), Schurmann's *Six Studies of Francis Bacon* and Shostakovich's Tenth Symphony. When the orchestra played the Shostakovich in London, Alan Blyth wrote in the *Daily Telegraph*: 'The Hallé under James Loughran proved itself high in the pecking order of British orchestras . . . It yielded practically nothing to performances by its supposedly more virtuoso brethren . . . The support for Joaquin Achucarro in Rachmaninov's *Rhapsody on a Theme of Paganini* was just as accomplished.' Blyth singled out the Hallé's principal horn, Michael Purton, for special praise, and no wonder. The biggest single undertaking was by Maurice Handford, with Penderecki's *St Luke Passion* of 1966 on 23 March 1980. John Ireland's centenary was marked by the Piano Concerto (Philip Fowke) and Frank Bridge's by *The Sea*. Walter Süsskind revived Strauss's *Alpine Symphony* (absent from the Hallé since 1923) on 11 October 1979, Witold Rowicki conducted Tadeusz Baird's *Four Novelettes* (22 November), Groves conducted the first Hallé performance on 6 December 1979 of Tippett's Fourth Symphony, Ždenek Macal brought Martinu's Fourth Piano Concerto, and Sergiu Comissiona, with Leon Fleischer as solo pianist, at last introduced Britten's *Diversions* (1940) for left-hand to Manchester. György Lehel, Gaetano Delogu, Marc Soustrot and Hans-Hubert Schönzeler were among other guest conductors. And, of course, Yansons who, besides Shostakovich's Eighth Symphony, revived Rossini's lovely *Stabat Mater*, with Felicity Lott, Alfreda Hodgson, Graham Clark and Stafford Dean as the soloists with the Hallé Choir, and conducted it, the *Telegraph* critic said, with 'the sparkle, intensity and Mediterranean glow usually associated with the composer's compatriots'. The eightieth anniversary of Barbirolli's birth was remembered on 2 December 1979 when Groves conducted Vaughan Williams's Eighth Symphony and Elgar's *The Music Makers* (soloist, Alfreda Hodgson). When the L.S.O. under Claudio Abbado played Schubert, Mozart and Brahms in Manchester on 14 October, the ovation for Michael Davis as leader exceeded that for the conductor! Among the season's solo pianists were Curzon (now Sir Clifford), Peter Frankl, Cristina Ortiz, Alicia de Larrocha, Anne Queffélec, Dmitri Alexeev and Peter Donohoe, while the violinists included Miriam Fried and Shlomo Mintz. The Salzburg Mozarteum and Leipzig Gewandhaus Bach Orchestras gave Mozart and Bach concerts respectively and, on 1 May, Giulini conducted the Los Angeles Philharmonic in the Adagio from Mahler's Tenth Symphony and Beethoven's 'Eroica'.

The Hallé entered the 1980s having increased in size from ninety-three at the time of Barbirolli's death in 1970 to a hundred. The annual cost of maintaining the orchestra had risen in a decade from £350,000 to almost £1½ million. Society membership had risen from under 1,500 to over 4,000 and where there was one regular sponsor in 1970 – Wilson's Brewery – in 1980 there were twelve. Life membership of the Society, unchanged at £100 since 1899, was increased to £350. Corporate membership, a new category for companies, was introduced in 1980 at a fee of £500. The founder corporate members were Barclays Bank, B.A.S.F. United Kingdom, Charlton Seal Dimmock and Co., General Site Services, Granada Television, I.C.I. (Pharmaceuticals Division), and Wilson's Brewery. The frightening rate of inflation in the 1970s affected the financial status of every artistic organisation in the country. Undoubtedly it also led programme-planners to err on the side of caution. The Hallé's principal fear was that, as had been its complaint for over thirty years, it was penalised for its success. Its deficit on the 1979-80 season was £19,388. It gave 156 public concerts and undertook fifty-six other engagements (broadcasts, recording and school concerts). For 1980 it faced a deficit of £120,000. Smart was especially critical of the Arts Council's attitude. 'Given that we have our own way of financing the Hallé,' he said in September 1980, 'the attitude that people seem to be taking is that "as you have done very well in the past, we will give you less in the future". It is this that in one fell swoop has created this situation.' In six years since 1974 the Arts Council's grant from the Treasury had risen by 230 per cent while the retail price index had risen by 150 per cent. In the same period the regional orchestras had received increases in grants amounting to 110 per cent while the Hallé increase had been 74 per cent. Although the Arts Council denied the charge of unfairness, it announced in February 1981 that for 1981-2 its grant to the Hallé would be increased by £59,000 to £354,000. G.M.C.'s grant was £303,000.

The 1980-1 season, Loughran's tenth, opened in Manchester on 6 September, at the Royal Northern College of Music (formed in 1972 after amalgamation of the Royal Manchester College and Northern School of Music). Handford conducted sessions of rehearsals, performances and discussions to select a composer to write a work for the 125th season in 1982-3. Paul Dewhirst of the *Daily Telegraph* would have voted, he wrote, for Christopher Brown, but the judges, Handford, Paul Patterson and John McCabe, unanimously chose Gary Carpenter, whose *Concerto for Orchestra* had been played. Loughran opened the Free Trade Hall season with Bruckner's Fourth Symphony (also performed in mid-season) and closed it with his Ninth. Other works he conducted were Elgar's First Symphony, *Enigma Variations*, Cello Concerto (Colin Carr) and Violin Concerto (twice, with Nigel Kennedy and Menuhin), Walton's Viola Concerto (Nobuko Imai), Dvořák's Sixth Symphony, and Berg's Three Orchestral Pieces. To mark the centenary of Bartók's birth, the *Concerto for Orchestra* (Kamu), *Dance Suite* (Loughran) and Second Violin Concerto (Menuhin and Loughran) were played. Not before time, Deryck Cooke's performing version of Mahler's Tenth Symphony, already played in Manchester at a B.B.C. Master Concert, was included in the Hallé season, although a strike by municipal employees forced closure of the Free Trade Hall on Thursday, 20 November, and the performance – which was to be broadcast – was given from the B.B.C.'s new Studio 7. The performance in the Free Trade Hall three days later did more justice to the work and to Stanislaw Skrowaczewski's interpretation. Kamu conducted the first British performance of Sallinen's Fourth Symphony (23 October), Groves restored Vaughan Williams's Fourth Symphony, Janet Baker sang Chausson's *Poème de l'amour et de la mer*, with Marc Soustrot conducting, Handford conducted McCabe's Third Piano Concerto with the composer as soloist, and Elgar's *The Dream of Gerontius*, James Conlon conducted two performances of Liszt's *Faust Symphony*, Mark Elder conducted Walton's *Belshazzar's Feast* and Yansons revived Scriabin's *Poem of Ecstasy*.

From 25 January to 21 February 1981 the Hallé was on tour in Hong Kong and Australia. Of its ten concerts at the ninth Hong Kong Festival, six were conducted by Loughran and four by Handford. McCabe's *Hartmann Variations* and Third Piano Concerto, Elgar's *Enigma Variations, In the South*, Violin Concerto (Nigel Kennedy) and First Symphony, Strauss's *Four Last Songs* (Anne Edwards) and *Till Eulenspiegel*, and Beethoven's Triple Concerto were among the works played. The Hallé was given a rapturous welcome on its second visit to the festival – 'as vibrant as ever' was one verdict, 'the tone still has that indefinable Hallé quality, fruity, full of bonhomie and very compelling'. Philip Radcliffe, of Manchester University and the *Daily Mail*, wrote (in the *Hallé Year Book* 1981-2) that no one who was there would forget 'the sight and sound of a predominantly Chinese audience clapping rhythmically while the Hallé played Viennese pieces, the Strauss waltzes and the polkas, urged on by James Loughran. There we were, 6,500 miles from home, not even in cosmopolitan Hong Kong proper, but breaking new ground, on a cultural mission really, up in the New Territories, in Tsuen Wan new town, and the audience, newly exposed to this kind of music, was completely caught up in the sheer enjoyment of it all. The band could have played all night as far as these Chinese fans were concerned.' In Australia, the Hallé played in Sydney, Melbourne, Adelaide and Perth, a total of eight concerts all conducted by Loughran, in the hottest summer on record. The Elgar works and Bruckner's Fourth Symphony were the backbone of the programmes. The *Sydney Morning Herald* critic thought Loughran 'need fear no comparison with his famous predecessor Barbirolli', while the critic of *The Australian* singled out the playing of the Elgar symphony for 'supremely musical and finely balanced sound'. The leading Melbourne critic described the Hallé's two concerts there as 'a source of jubilant pleasure. Here is an orchestra which plays with what seems to be instinctive balance.' An Adelaide writer referred to the string tone as 'mellow, full-bodied and warm as good English dark ale'. An English critic with long experience of the Hallé, Ernest Bradbury, described the tour as 'an artistic triumph . . . a thrilling, exhilarating and indeed privileged time, a February to remember'.

In the Hallé's absence on its longest and most successful tour, Manchester was visited by the R.L.P.O., the English Chamber Orchestra in a Mozart programme with Maurizio Pollini as conductor/pianist, the Polish National Symphony Orchestra, and its own chamber orchestra, the Camerata, which was joined by a disproportionately large Hallé Choir for Haydn's *Nelson Mass*, conducted by Meredith Davies. The season ended with a visit from the Concertgebouw Orchestra of Amsterdam, under Haitink, with Shostakovich's Fifth Symphony as the main offering. Perhaps the most notable of the new soloists was the violinist Eugene Sarbu, but the outstanding memory is of Menuhin's superb and moving playing of the concertos of Bartók and Elgar. Of the latter the *Daily Telegraph* critic wrote: 'What was unforgettable was the extraordinarily beautiful sound Menuhin conjured from the violin in those passages where Elgar bares to us the instrument's soul as well as his own, and the unique understanding he has of the structure of the work, when to press forward and when to hold back, when to catch the breath (and stop our heart in the process) and when to release the flood of oratory. He has long since handed on the torch to younger violinists where infallibility of technique is concerned in this work, but the steady glow with which he illuminates its poetry and passion is his secret, imparted to him by Edward Elgar. Mr Loughran and the orchestra provided a superb backcloth and their playing of the *Eroica* was that of a great orchestra.'

During the 1980-1 season the Hallé gave 146 public concerts, undertook thirty-three other engagements and gave eighteen concerts on its foreign tour. The result artistically was good; financially it was the largest deficit in the Society's history, £92,346. Smart again turned his fire on the Arts Council. The increase in grant to the Hallé was still £60,000 less than had been offered to the Liverpool and Birmingham orchestras, he pointed out. The Hallé had earned almost sixty per cent of its expenditure, much more than any other regional orchestra had achieved. He recognised the Council's problems in trying to operate within the limits of the Government's strict policy, but the Hallé's own financial performance showed that it too had recognised the part it must play in times of economic stringency. For 1981-2 the Arts Council increased its grant by £65,000 to £360,000, with a further £34,000 towards any deficit incurred during the year.

Enthusiasm for the 1981-2 Manchester programmes was difficult to muster. These were announced to the public in a new form, a 'give-away' leaflet. This was followed later by a *Year Book* which took the place of the prospectus of former years and of the *Hallé* magazine. The *Hallé News* was instituted to give information at intervals throughout the year. The first *Year Book* contained articles on the Hong Kong and Australian tour, on the programmes, on Haydn Symphonies by Gerald Larner, and on Tippett by Leonard Duck, recently retired Librarian of the Henry Watson Music Library and a valued writer of many of the Hallé's most searching analytical notes. One of the few contemporary works performed during the season was Tippett's Triple Concerto (21 January 1982), conducted by Loughran with the three soloists who had given the first performance in 1980, György Pauk (violin), Nobuko Imai (viola) and Ralph Kirshbaum (cello). Akeo Watanabe conducted Takemitsu's *Marginalia* ('harmless modern music without tears, and only ten minutes long', wrote Paul Dewhirst). György Lehel conducted Rudolf Maros's *Notices* for strings. The 250th anniversary of Haydn's birth was saluted by performances of the last six Salomon Symphonies, Nos. 99-104, and the 80th of Walton's by the First Symphony and the *Hindemith Variations*. Loughran conducted two Mahler symphonies, Nos. 4 and 9, Yansons Shostakovich's Ninth and Rachmaninov's Second, and Groves Nielsen's Fifth and Tippett's *Child of Our Time*. Among the unscheduled soloists were Régine Crespin, who took Janet Baker's place when she was ill in February, and Ian Hobson, winner of the 1981 Leeds piano competition, who substituted for Pascal Rogé. At the Proms in July, history repeated itself when, as with Ogdon in 1962, a Manchester-trained pianist, Peter Donohoe, returned from his joint silver medal success at the Moscow Tchaikovsky competition to play Rachmaninov's *Paganini Rhapsody*.

At the height of the season an event occurred news of which, if it reached the spirits of Godlee and Barbirolli, would have assured them that nothing much had changed in Manchester. Using the Government's insistence on cuts in extravagant municipal budgets as a political excuse, Manchester City Council's cultural committee decided to recommend the city council to withdraw the whole of the £30,000 grant to the Hallé (unchanged since 1974). At the same time, the charge for renting the Free Trade Hall was increased by over a hundred per cent, from between £250 and £300 a day depending on the day of the

The Hallé on tour: (*above*) Sir John, Lady Barbirolli and the Lord Mayor of Manchester, Alderman Harold Stockdale, with the Orchestra at Ringway Airport in June 1968 before leaving for South America; (*below*) playing at the Athens Festival in 1961

week to between £500 and £700. Eventually the council relented and
reduced the grant by a third, to £20,000. That this had little to do with
culture or economy was shown by the council's decision to spend
£90,000 on its own 'international festival' in September 1982 even
though its previous events of this kind had been disastrous financial
and artistic failures. The result, for the Hallé, was cancellation of one of
the summer Proms and a reduction in the numbers of concerts in the
1982-3 season in Manchester.

The council's final decision was taken on 1 March 1982. On 29 April
James Loughran announced that he was to relinquish his Hallé post at
the end of the 125th season in the summer of 1983. He was also to leave
his Bamberg post at the same time. His association with the Hallé
would continue and the Society invited him to become Conductor
Laureate from the 1983-4 season. He had achieved a notable period of
thorough consolidation. It cannot have been easy to follow a great man
who was also something of a folk-hero, yet he rebuilt the orchestra,
attracted some brilliant new principals, made recordings which won
almost unanimous acclaim, gave greater prominence to the work of the
Hallé Choir and maintained audiences at a high level. Many young
couples in his audiences today probably never heard Barbirolli in
person; to them, the Hallé was Loughran's orchestra. His conducting
of the symphonies of Beethoven and Bruckner had a special
distinction, but he was perhaps unduly modest about coming forward
as a champion of any particular composer or group of composers.
When, after the announcement of his decision, he conducted Mahler's
Ninth Symphony in Manchester, he was warmly acclaimed. The *Daily
Telegraph* critic wrote that 'the performance . . . was so technically
accomplished that it was as if he was saying: "I have kept your
orchestra in good repair and trained a new generation of fine young
players to continue the tradition." Let us hope the 125th season will be
a worthy tribute to his achievements.'

The programmes Loughran and Smart devised for the 125th season
showed a flair for combining historical significance with box-office
attraction. Loughran chose to conduct two of the great choral
masterpieces Hallé introduced to Manchester, Beethoven's Mass in D
and Verdi's *Requiem*. Hallé's championship of Brahms, Dvořák and
Tchaikovsky was saluted, and of course his devotion to Berlioz. Harty
and Barbirolli were remembered through Mahler – the First, Third and

Fifth Symphonies and *Das Lied von der Erde* – and Vaughan Williams (Eighth Symphony). Elgar – the *Enigma Variations* and Second Symphony – and Strauss – *Ein Heldenleben* – marked the Richter era. No Bruckner, oddly enough, and very little Sibelius, but contemporary works by Kokkonen (Fourth Symphony), Lutoslawski (Concerto for oboe and harp), David Wooldridge (*Five Italian Songs*), Skrowaczewski (Clarinet Concerto), McCabe (*Music's Empire*), and Goehr (*Deux Etudes*); and, of course, the commissioned work by Gary Carpenter, *Amethyst Deceiver*. With Yansons conducting Shostakovich's Fourth Symphony and soloists like Ashkenazy (in Bartók's Second Piano Concerto), Radu Lupu, Nathan Milstein, Cécile Ousset, Stephen Hough, Nigel Kennedy, Imogen Cooper, Heinz Holliger and several from the orchestra itself, the programmes contrived to look back and to look ahead. For the 125th birthday concert itself, on 30 January 1983, the chosen soloist in Beethoven's Fourth Concerto was that prince of pianists, Sir Clifford Curzon, a link with the first week of Barbirolli's Hallé and the centenary night. Alas, he died in the previous September.

For any orchestral organisation, the perennial problem must be to reconcile the need to pay its way at the box-office with the need to introduce new works and to broaden the audience's musical horizon. There is an alarming gap, seemingly wider than ever today, between the professional critic's craving for enterprise and the general public's capacity to accept it. With so much music available on the radio and on record, with the means to study difficult or unfamiliar works so much more easily accessible than it was in the past, it is depressing that the average member of the concert audience, not only in Manchester, is so unwilling to lend an attentive ear to the vast majority of twentieth-century works – though it has to be conceded that many composers make little or no effort to woo the public. The managements' reply to criticism of 'conservative' programmes was cogently put by Sir Francis Tombs, chairman-elect of the Association of British Orchestras, in London on 14 June 1982: 'It is now a truism, but that does not make it less important to repeat – there are always large numbers in our audiences who are coming for the first time to the great classics of the repertoire . . . The orchestras make no apology for devoting a considerable amount of their time to performing the standard and central classical repertoire . . . It is no service to the composer to put on an ill-prepared and under-rehearsed performance of a new work. The proper presentation of new music at regular intervals, with each piece given more than one performance, is costly and the problem of attracting audiences cannot be ignored.'

Money, then, is the key to the future for the Hallé Orchestra, if it is to revert to the enterprising proselytizing of its founder's era and if it is to retain the right players. The Society is due for another period when it must take risks and be bold, for if history shows anything it shows that that is when the Hallé has reached the heights. What it needs is a strong conductor willing, if and when necessary, to fight the committee and the management for what he believes, or, better still, able to inflame them with a sense of 'mission'. If he is in the true Hallé tradition, the audience will willingly follow him into uncharted domains. In present-day economic conditions the real danger is that the Hallé could become merely another provincial orchestra. In that case, it might as well be the Manchester Philharmonic. But the very name Hallé implies individuality and a cosmopolitan outlook and ambition. That is the only sure road to success – and survival. The next conductor must be able to say, as John Barbirolli said in 1946, 'I should like to feel we are on the verge of great things.'

Select bibliography

Batley, Thomas (editor), *Sir Charles Hallé's Concerts in Manchester*: a list of vocal and instrumental soloists and programmes of concerts, 1858-95 (Manchester, 1896).

Cardus, Sir Neville, *The Delights of Music: a critic's choice* (London, 1966).

Freer, David (editor), *Hamilton Harty, Early Memoirs* (Belfast, 1979); *Hamilton Harty, his Life and Music* (Belfast, 1979).

Hallé Magazine, 1946-81 (Manchester, Hallé Club and Hallé Concerts Society).

Jefferson, Alan, *Sir Thomas Beecham* (London, 1979).

Kennedy, Michael, *The Hallé Tradition* (Manchester, 1960); *Barbirolli: Conductor Laureate* (London, 1971); (editor), *The Autobiography of Charles Hallé* (London, 1972).

Kenyon, Nicholas, *The B.B.C. Symphony Orchestra: the first fifty years, 1930-80* (London, 1981).

Reid, Charles, *John Barbirolli* (London, 1971).

Russell, John F., *A History of the Hallé Concerts, 1858-1939* (serialised in the *Hallé Magazine*, Manchester, 1948-56).

Valuable documentation of the Barbirolli era is contained in the first two recordings issued by the Barbirolli Society (BS01 and BS02) in which Sir John speaks about his career.

Index

145

146

147

The Sponsors and Corporate Members of the Hallé Concerts Society

include the following –

Barclays Bank plc.
BASF United Kingdom
   Limited
British Engine Insurance
Colgate-Palmolive Limited
Hambros Bank Limited
ICI plc.
Mr John Morris Jones
Pernod
Piccadilly Radio
Price Waterhouse
Rank Xerox (UK) Limited
Thomas French plc.
Williams & Glyn's Bank plc.
Wilsons Brewery Limited
Granada Television Limited
G T Management Limited
IBM United Kingdom Limited
Lloyds Bank
Martini & Rossi
Mobil
National Westminster Bank

Noilly Prat
Richard Bates Limited
Boardman Securities
Charlton Seal Dimmock and
   Company
Foysters
General Site Services Limited
Gordon Emery Limited
ICI plc Pharmaceuticals
   Division
ICI plc Wallcoverings Group
Lanchester Taverns
Manchester Evening News
   Limited
Norwest Holst Limited
Ove Arup Partnership
P A Management Consultants
   Limited
Raab Karcher (UK) Limited
Refuge Assurance
The Scottish Life Assurance
   Company